A1SB

An A1 Sporting Books publication
in association with NMG Publishing
© Terry Baker/Norman Giller/Michael Giller 2010

First published in 2010 by A1 Sporting Books
Unit 20, 12 Airfield Road, Christchurch, Dorset. BH23 3TQ

10 9 8 7 6 5 4 3 2 1

A CIP catalogue for this title is available from the British Library
ISBN 978-0-9543243-9-1
Typeset and designed by NMG Publishing, Dorset, UK
Printed and bound in the United Kingdom by Antony Rowe Limited
Bumper's Farm, Chippenham, Wiltshire SN14 6LH

*The Publisher and authors give special thanks for their efficiency and friendly co-operation
to the Antony Rowe team, and in particular to Chris Jones, Mark Radley,
Geoff Fisher and Dave Biggs*

GREAVSIE'S GREATEST

**The 50 greatest British goalscorers
of the last 50 years – selected
by the greatest of them all**

NORMAN GILLER and TERRY BAKER

Edited by Michael Giller

Illustrations: Art Turner

A1SB

Art Turner
2010

Dedicated to the memory
of Bobby Smith, one of the
great goalscorers
1933-2010

Greavsie's Greatest: *Contents*

SELECT your fifty greatest British goalscorers of the last fifty years was the challenge from publisher, promoter, my good mate and agent, Terry Baker. Easy-peasy I thought as I got my pencil out and started writing down names. First of all I listed my schoolboy idols Tommy Lawton, Tom Finney, Billy Liddell and Raich Carter. Terry looked over my shoulder and shook his head. "I said the last fifty years, not seventy," he said, not caring that he was wiping off the map four of the greatest footballers I ever saw.

When he also disallowed Nat Lofthouse, Jackie Milburn, Stan Mortensen and John Charles I realised it was not going to be as simple as I thought. He peered over my shoulder a while later and shook his head again as I listed modern greats Glenn Hoddle, Paul Gascoigne, Ryan Giggs, Frank Lampard, Steven Gerrard, David Beckham and Paul Scholes.

"They have to be specialist strikers," he instructed. "Not wingers or midfield players. I want to publish a book that gives the out-and-out British goal strikers the credit they deserve. With all the foreigners now invading the game they are almost becoming a dying breed at the top level." He allowed me George Best and Bobby Charlton when I threatened to decapitate him if they were not in my top 50 British goalscorers list.

I called in Team Giller to help me – Norman, a prolific writer who has been my partner in 19 books, and his sports statistician son, Michael, who knows all the facts and figures most of the rest of us can only guess at. I was never one for counting goals. I was too busy trying to score them. So the facts of this book have been provided by the Gillers, but the all-important *feelings* are mine.

Please play along with me and see how many of my selections you agree with. I know my choices will start more arguments than they'll settle, but it is opinions that make the football world go round, and if the book gets you debating my selections with your mates then we've achieved our target of making you think beyond the pages.

The game today is, uh, foreign to me. There is not a Premier League club that does not have a playing staff stuffed with overseas players. They bring colour, technique and talent to our football, but it means British footballers are hardly getting a chance to show what they can do. The time is not far off when the England football manager will have to go to reserve games to find his players.

So it's good to have this opportunity to salute the fifty greatest British goalscorers of the last fifty yeats. It reminds us that we can produce players who know how to hit the back of the net. See if you agree with my selections. Let the arguments begin!

Greatest Of Them All by *TERRY BAKER*

W HO'S the Greatest? It is one of the most popular of all sporting topics, and I have long wanted to publish a book that ends the arguments as to who have been the greatest British goalscorers of the last fifty years. Who better to ask, I thought, than without doubt the greatest of them all – James Peter Greaves.

Jimmy, a legend I am proud and privileged to represent and to introduce and interview in our long-running road shows, is one of the most modest men I know. His next boast will be his first. Let me blow the trumpet for him: he scored an all-time record 357 First Division goals, still holds the Tottenham record of 220 League goals, netted a mind-boggling 492 goals in all senior matches before retiring at the premature age of thirty-one ... and on the international stage he banged in 44 goals for England in just 57 matches (Bobby Charlton's all-time record 49 goals came in 106 games).

He is the ideal man to name the fifty greatest British goalscorers of the last fifty years. Turn the clock back fifty years and teenager Jimmy was already established as a prolific goalscorer. He made his debut for Chelsea in 1957 at the age of 17, and scored against Tottenham at White Hart Lane at the start of a sensational goal rush that lasted until his far-too-early retirement in 1971 at the age of just 31.

Jimmy was involved right at the heart of the game as a player for fifteen years, and remained with his finger on the pulse throughout the Eighties and Nineties as one of the most popular of all television pundits, usually in harness with Ian St John. ITV's ending of the Saint and Greavsie show was a huge own goal, in my opinion. Since then Jimmy has become one of the finest stand-up comedians in the land and, as anybody who attends our road shows will know, has blistering opinions on the state of the game today.

My A1 Sporting Books publishing company – specialising in sports nostalgia – is delighted to present this all-embracing record of the greatest British goalscorers. I know it will appeal to those who like to wallow in football nostalgia, and it will serve as evidence to the younger generation that we have produced many outstanding marksmen, and that we have not always leaned on overseas stars like Thierry Henry, Cristiano Ronaldo and Didier Drogba to find the net. This book – Jimmy's book – will prove it. Enjoy!

Terry Baker

Jimmy shows off his 1966 World Cup medal at Downing Street, with Terry Baker sharing the moment

Play the Selecting Game by Norman Giller

IF you want to join in the selecting game with Greavsie, the rules are simple. The fifty players you pick must be 1) British born; 2) A specialist striker (which, in the main, rules out wingers and midfielders); 3) They must have played during the last 50 years, going back to when Spurs won the League title and FA Cup double in 1960-61.

We are presenting Jimmy's choices in the order of their birth, and we both found it extremely moving that his first selection was his old Spurs side-kick Bobby Smith in the very week that our mutual friend passed on at the age of 77.

Jimmy and I both agreed that we should dedicate the book to the memory of Bobby. Together, they were dynamic for Tottenham and England. We used to say: "Bobby'll knock 'em down, Jimmy'll knock 'em in."

Thanks to my many years reporting from the football press boxes and dressing-rooms, we are able to give the added bonus of quotes from the fifty featured players on the greatest goals that they scored. Most were collected and collated for articles written for newspapers and magazines, particularly during my years as chief football reporter for the *Daily Express*. Extra quotes have been provided by Fleet Street colleagues, for which I thank them. Thanks, too, to graphics artist Art Turner for his stunning illustrations.

You will rarely find a book like this with so many informative stats on British goalscorers. My son, right-hand man, partner and best friend Michael has furnished all the statistical data that gives a strong foundation to the expert opinions and comments of the one and only Greavsie.

This is the 20th book that Jimmy and I have collaborated on, and it has given us a bigger headache than several of the others put together. The problem was not so much deciding who to put in as which players to leave out. It was tough for both of us to have to omit forwards of the calibre of Bob Latchford, Paul Mariner, Stuart Pearson, Lou Macari, Peter Crouch and so many more. But the rules are: just 50 players, no more, no less. Now it's over to Jimmy. It's better than fifty50 that he will score with you.

Jimmy Greaves, the Artful Dodger of the penalty area

FACTFILE: Born: Co Durham, February 22 1933
Died: Enfield, September 19 2010
Career span: 1950-65. Had his peak years with Spurs,
shooting them to the League and Cup double in 1960-61 with
33 goals, and picked up a second successive FA Cup winners' medal in 1962. Started his career with Chelsea and
finished in the League with Brighton before joining Hast-
ings. Bagged 13 goals in 15 England games, and his total
League haul was 217 from 376 matches. He had two great
partnerships, first with Les Allen and then Greavsie.

GREAVSIE ASSESSMENT : `I feel very emotional discussing Bobby, because we just heard of his passing as we prepared this very page. He was my favourite centre-forward partner. He was never given the credit he deserved for his high level of skill. People seemed to think he was all brute force. Strength certainly played a big part in his game, and he used to make full use of his heavyweight physique, but he also had subtle touches and could lay off delicate passes.

I fed off him at Spurs and with England, and am pleased to acknowledge the part he played in my goal accumulation. He used to win the ball for me in the air, remove a defender or two with the sheer force of his challenge and I was left with the relatively simple job of finishing the move. Wonder if he'll find a betting shop Up There? He did love a punt. Bobby was a bit of a rascal but lovable with it. I will miss lovely old Smithy.´

BOBBY SMITH'S Most Memorable Goal

MATCH: Tottenham v. Leicester City
SEASON: 1960-61, FA Cup final

⁶It was the 69th minute of the match and Leicester's defence had been frustrating us. Then I managed to break the scoring deadlock when Terry Dyson pierced the defence with a neat through ball. I wrong-footed the Leicester defenders with a feint and then swivelled to score with a shot on the turn from fifteen yards. Gordon Banks dived full length but couldn't get a touch as the ball flashed into the corner of the net. Seven minutes later I returned the compliment to Terry Dyson when I found him with a cross that he headed into the net at the far post. What made it all so memorable was that the win made us the first team of the century to complete the League and Cup double.⁹

Graphics artist Art Turner captures Bobby Smith challenging Wolves goalkeeper Malcolm Finlayson circa 1961, and the inset illustration shows Bobby in his prime at Tottenham

Gerry Hitchens and Greavsie in friendly mood before an Inter-AC Milan derby in 1961

FACTFILE: Born Rawnsley, Staffs, October 8 1934
Died: Clwyd, Wales, April 13 1983
Career span: 1955-69. Had his peak years in Italy with
Inter-Milan, Torino, Atalanta and Cagliari. His nine-
year stay in Italy is a record for a British footballer.
Started with Kidderminster, and scored 118 League goals
for Cardiff and Aston Villa before his move to Italy in
1961. Netted 23 times for Villa's 1959-60 Second Division
title team. Capped seven times by England, five goals.
Returned home in 1969 and played for Worcester City.

GREAVSIE ASSESSMENT: `I admired the way Gerry stuck it out in Italy during a defence-dominated era when – and I speak from experience – life was tough for strikers. He was not the most elegant of players, but had strength and courage and knew where the goal was. Give him a sniff, and the ball was in the net.

I played alongside Gerry in six of his seven England appearances, and found him a big-hearted and unselfish partner who was a handful for centre-halves with his dashing style of play.

We were good mates in Milan, despite playing for the rival clubs. The rules were that we should not consort with "the enemy", but we used to nip off for quiet drinks together. Football rescued Gerry from working in the coal mines, and it was the game's gain. A super player and a smashing bloke.´

GERRY HITCHENS' Most Memorable Goal
MATCH: Italy v. England
SEASON: Close-season, May 24 1961

•The press built the match up as the Championship of Europe. Six minutes before half-time Jimmy Armfield made one of his dangerous overlapping runs down the right, and I anticipated what he was going to do and drew clear of my two markers. Jimmy got his cross over to perfection and I jumped and met it with my head with full force. The ball flew into the top corner, and suddenly the crowd in Rome's Olympic Stadium was silenced. I scored again from a Jimmy Greaves pass ten minutes from the end to make it 2-2 and Greavsie then snatched a magical late winner. My performance persuaded Inter to buy me from Aston Villa, so the game did me a big favour.•

FACTFILE: Born Middlesbrough, March 21 1935
Died: Derby, September 20 2004
Career span: 1954-64. Netted 197 goals for Middlesbrough and 54 for Sunderland in a total of just 274 League games before a knee injury finished his career. Top Second Division scorer for three successive seasons, and capped twice by England. Later emerged as one of the greatest English managers of all time, steering Derby County to the League title in 1972 and Nottingham Forest to the title in 1978 and to two back-to-back European Cup triumphs.

GREAVSIE ASSESSMENT: `Cloughie was a dynamic and direct centre-forward who knew the shortest and surest way to goal. His eventful and stunningly successful career as a manager tended to overshadow the fact that he was a goal snatcher with few equals. He played his two England games with me alongside him, but the selectors did not give us enough time to gel and he was discarded after a draw with Wales and a 3-2 defeat by Sweden.

He deserved many more caps, but I think the establishment was frightened of his brutally honest views, which is also the way it was when he became the greatest manager never to manage England. His achievement, along with partner Peter Taylor, in guiding Nottingham Forest to two successive European Cup wins was just unbelievable. Adding to his legend was his 44 days in charge at Leeds when he was beaten by player power. There will never be another Cloughie. He really WAS the Special One´

BRIAN CLOUGH'S Most Memorable Goal

MATCH: Wolves v. Middlesbrough
SEASON: 1951-52, Intermediate match

`I intercepted a crossfield pass in my own half and ran to the edge of the Wolves penalty area in an inside-left position. I then struck a left-foot shot which hit the side of the net inside the far post. This is the goal that has stuck in my memory above all the others I scored at first-team level. I was only a youngster and the goal gave me an enormous feeling of having achieved something special. The fact that it was at Molineux, which was then one of the great cathedrals of English football, added to the wonder of it and that goal gave me the confidence to always go direct for the target. You never saw me pussyfoot around. I went straight for the jugular.`

Brian Clough, who was a prolific goalscorer for Middlesbrough and Sunderland

Father Les Allen and son Clive, relatively speaking exceptional marksmen

FACTFILE: Born Dagenham, September 4 1937
Career span: 1956-69. Payed for Chelsea, Tottenham and
QPR. An England Under-23 international, he joined Spurs
from Chelsea in a 1959 exchange deal involving Johnny
Brooks. Was an ever-present in Tottenham's 'Double' winning team of 1960-61, scoring 23 First Division goals. He
then pulled off another double with QPR, helping them win
the Third Division title and the League Cup in 1966-67.
The previous season he was top Third Division marksman
with 30 goals. Later managed QPR and Swindon.

GREAVSIE ASSESSMENT: `Les was alongside me when I made my League debut for Chelsea, and again when I played my first match for Spurs. He was a neat, constructive centre-forward or inside-forward, with a fine turn of speed, an accurate shot with either foot and excellent positional sense.

We tossed up as to which Allen would get into my Top 50, because his son Clive was an equally fine goalscorer who hit a purple patch with Spurs in the 1986-87 season when he scored an astonishing 49 goals in all competitions. This was more than his Dad – more than almost anybody – ever achieved in a single season.

There were Allens galore playing football in Dagenham when I was a youngster playing my schools football in that area, and Les did the family proud with his achievements. As well as his skill, he had a good temperament, and was respected for his sportsmanship and total commitment.´

LES ALLEN'S Most Memorable Goal
MATCH: Wolves v. Tottenham
SEASON: 1960-61, First Division

❛Seven Spurs players were involved in a series of first-time passes that tore the Wolves defence apart. The ball was played to me from the right by John White just outside the box. I ran on to it and hammered it into the top corner of the net. It was one-touch magic, and the third goal in a 4-0 victory against the old champions on their own turf. It was our eleventh successive victory since the start of the season, a record that will take some beating. We virtually had the League championship wrapped up by Christmas, and went on to become the first team of the 20th Century to complete the League and FA Cup double. It was a joy to play for that team.❜

FACTFILE: Born Ashington, October 11 1937
Career span: 1956-75. He set two club records with Manchester United – 198 goals in 606 League matches. His honours haul included winners' medals in the World Cup (1966), European Cup (1968), League championship (1957-65-67) and FA Cup (1963). Holds the all-time goalscoring record for England, 49 goals in 106 games. European Footballer of the Year and FWA Footballer of the Year in 1966, and knighted in 1994. Was briefly player-manager of Preston and lifted his League goals tally to 206.

GREAVSIE ASSESSMENT: `Bobby mercifully survived the 1958 Munich air crash to become a legend in his own lifetime. Britain has never had a greater sporting ambassador. His performances on the pitch and his demeanour off it made him loved and respected throughout the world. I shall go so far as to say he rivals even Churchill as the best known Briton of my lifetime.

Bobby was a household name just everywhere I travelled with him in the world. He was dynamic for England and Man United as a blond left-winger and inside-forward before becoming a balding midfield director, wrecking defences with his inch-perfect passes and bombshell shooting.

He and his big brother Jack won World Cup honours together, yet were alike as grass and granite. Bobby was quiet and often withdrawn, while Jackie always had lots to say for himself. They gave England and their clubs – Jack at Leeds – wonderful service.´

BOBBY CHARLTON'S Most Memorable Goal
MATCH: Aston Villa v. Manchester United
SEASON: 1964-65, First Division

`There were goals in the World Cup and European Cup that gave me satisfaction in my heart, but it is a pretty meaningless goal in the First Division that has stayed in my memory. We had already won the League championship and were 2-0 down in this final game of the season at Villa Park. I picked the ball up on the halfway line, took it past five players and then squeezed a shot just inside the post. It was the build-up to the goal that gave me lasting satisfaction. The following season I was privileged to be part of the England team that won the World Cup and two seasons later I helped United win the European Cup. You could say they were good times!´

Bobby Charlton, the shining knight of English football

Ian St John, an artist of a centre-forward for Liverpool and Scotland

Greavsie's Greatest: 6. IAN ST JOHN

FACTFILE: Born Motherwell, June 7 1938
Career span: 1957-72. He was Motherwell's top scorer
three times in his first four seasons. Joined Liverpool in
1961 for £37,500 and became an idol of the Kop, winning a
Second Division championship medal in his first season at
Anfield. Collected First Division championship medals in
1964 and 1966, and scored the goal that won the FA Cup for
Liverpool in 1965. Capped 21 times by Scotland. Netted 178
League goals, played for Coventry and had brief spells in
management before becoming a TV personality.

GREAVSIE ASSESSMENT: `Saint was an artist of a centre-forward in the best Scottish traditions, holding his line together with intelligent positional play and neat flick passes. He and Roger Hunt were dynamic together.

Ian was such a hero at Anfield that when a local church displayed a poster asking, 'What would you do if Jesus returned among us?" somebody scrawled the answer, "Move St John to inside-left."

He later gave Liverpool skilled service from a midfield base, when his artful passing unlocked the tightest defences. Saint knew football inside out, and gained management experience with Motherwell and Portsmouth, as well as coaching and playing in South Africa.

It was football's loss when he chose a career in broadcasting. We had a great screen partnership, and our *Saint and Greavsie* show gave Ian the chance to reveal his in-depth knowledge of the game.´

IAN ST JOHN'S Most Memorable Goal

MATCH: Liverpool v. Leeds at Wembley
SEASON: 1965 FA Cup final

•It was nine minutes from the end of extra-time and the score was deadlocked at 1-1. Ian Callaghan found the strength and stamina to drive down the wing and fire over a powerful cross. The ball looked to be going behind me but I twisted and flung myself back and managed to get my head to it and steer it over the goal-line. You can't have a more memorable moment than scoring a winning goal for Liverpool at Wembley. It won the FA Cup for Liverpool for the first time, and the parties on Merseyside lasted for days. Even now, all these years later, supporters mention the goal to me as if I scored it yesterday.•

FACTFILE: Born Golborne, July 20 1938
Career span: 1959-72. Scored a Liverpool club record
245 League goals between 1959 and 1969. Added another
25 goals to his collection in two seasons with Bolton
before retiring to concentrate on his family road haulage
business. Won a Second Division championship medal in
1962, and was a key member of the Liverpool team that won
the League title in 1964 and 1966, and the FA Cup in 1965.
Helped England lift the World Cup in 1966, and scored 18
goals in 34 international matches.

GREAVSIE ASSESSMENT: `Roger's selfless running off the ball made him an invaluable team member, and his control and killer instinct in the penalty box meant he was also a devastating individual player. He and Ian St John were a perfect foil for each other, and when feeding off the wing play of Ian Callaghan and Steve Heighway were as dangerous a duo as there was in the 'old' First Division.

Legendary manager Bill Shankly summed Roger up beautifully when he said that he was a heart on legs. He would run marathon distances at sprint speed, always with the team targets in mind rather than any individual glory. He was strong, brave, quick and totally committed to every match. There was a healthy rivalry between Roger and myself for a place in the England attack, but it never interfered with our friendship. He was a good sportsman as well as being a great player. In short, I was a Roger Hunt fan.´

ROGER HUNT'S Most Memorable Goal
MATCH: Liverpool v. Leicester City
SEASON: 1964-65, FA Cup sixth round replay

❛I scored the only goal of the game late in the second-half. Chris Lawler crossed a long ball from the right touchline into the penalty area, where big Ron Yeats headed it down into my path. I connected with a crashing left-foot shot on the volley and the ball hit the stanchion in the back of the net and bounced back past that great goalkeeper Gordon Banks. It was memorable for me because Leicester had been our bogey team, and Banksie always seemed just unbeatable. We went on to win the FA Cup for the first time in the club's history – one of the most memorable days in my career at Wembley. Just over a year later I was back for the World Cup final. Happy days!❜

Roger Hunt, a heart on legs according to Bill Shankly

Alan Gilzean, all smoothness and skill for Spurs and Scotland

FACTFILE: Born Coupar Angus, October 23 1938
Career span: 1960-74. Gathered 113 goals with Dundee, and
was a leading marksman for them when they won the Scottish
League title for the first time in 1961-62. He once rattled
in seven goals for Dundee in a match against Queen of the
South in 1962. Transferred to Tottenham for £72,000 in
1964. Collected 93 League goals with Spurs, and picked up
an FA Cup winners' medal in 1967. Played in two winning
League Cup final teams (1971/73) and helped Spurs win the
Uefa Cup in 1972. Capped 23 times by Scotland.

GREAVSIE ASSESSMENT: `I considered myself fortunate to have a playing partner of Gillie's quality alongside me at Tottenham. He took over from Bobby Smith, playing a much more subtle game that was knitted with individual tricks that he had picked up while playing as a kid in Scotland. He told me: "There used to be about 20 players-a-side and just the one ball, so if you got hold of it you learned to dribble to make sure you kept it."

Gillie and I struck up an instant understanding when he arrived from Dundee and knew just what service to give each other to make the most of any situation. He was a master of the flick pass and glancing header, and was always graceful on the ball, no matter how great the pressure. A genius of a touch player. Everybody lost touch with Gillie, but it was great to hear that he had reappeared and was collecting awards up in Dundee for past glories. He was quite unique, both in style and substance.´

ALAN GILZEAN'S Most Memorable Goal

MATCH: Scotland v. England at Hampden Park
SEASON: 1963-64 Home Championship

`There was a gale-force wind blowing throughout the match and ball control was really difficult. We were deadlocked without a goal when we forced a corner on the left. Davie Wilson kicked it into the wind and I timed my jump just right and managed to head the ball wide of that fantastic goalkeeper Gordon Banks and into the back of the net for what turned out to be the only goal of the game. Later that year I was signed by Spurs, who had been keeping a close eye on me ever since that goal against England. I hate talking about my goals. I always saw it as my job to put the ball into the net, so I could never understand all the fuss.´

FACTFILE: Born West Horsley, May 18 1939
Died South Africa, October 27 1999
Career span: 1957-68. The first Fourth Division player
to win an England cap while with Crystal Palace, he had
his peak years with West Ham, winning an FA Cup winners'
medal in 1964. He was capped 11 times before a knee injury
wrecked his career. Returned briefly to Crystal Palace and
then had a season with Fulham. Scored 160 goals in 395
League games before emigrating to South Africa, where he
became a respected coach and manager.

GREAVSIE ASSESSMENT: `I warm at the memory of Johnny's company both on and off the pitch. He was a wonderfully gifted touch player who could infuriate central defenders with his clever ball play and deceptive changes of pace and direction. Not many people know it, but Johnny was pigeon-toed, which gave him four ways of playing the ball – with the inside and outside of both feet. We used to call him Budgie because he was always chatting. It was his Irish blood, he used to say. I don't think I've ever seen a better exponent of playing a first-time pass and then nipping away into position for the return.

He would have been a certainty for the 1966 World Cup squad but for damaging a knee while playing as an emergency defender against Scotland at Wembley in 1965. It virtually finished his career, and from then on he was never able to regain his old velvet touch that had made him just about untouchable.´

JOHNNY BYRNE'S Most Memorable Goal
MATCH: Lausanne v. West Ham
SEASON: 1964-65, European Cup Winners' Cup quarter-final

•We were under extreme pressure, clinging on to a slender lead we had earned in the first leg. I picked up the ball deep in our own half and ran virtually the length of the pitch, beating five of the Swiss players on the way. The pitch was heavy with clinging mud, and I was close to exhaustion as I reached the edge of the box. In sheer desperation I whacked the ball and then collapsed to the ground fighting for my breath. When I looked up, the Lausanne goalkeeper was bending down picking the ball out of the back of the net. We went on to win the match and, a few weeks later, captured the Cup Winners' Cup against Munich 1860 at Wembley.•

Johnny Byrne, a walking, talking ball master

Denis 'The Menace' Law, the original King of Old Trafford

> **FACTFILE:** Born Aberdeen, February 24 1940
> Career span: 1956-74. League debut with Huddersfield, aged 16. Scotland's youngest ever international in 1958, the first of 55 caps (30 goals). Joined Man City for a record £55,000 in 1960, then to Torino for £100,000 in 1961 and on to Man United for another record £115,000 in 1962. Scored 174 League goals for United in 309 matches and then returned to Man City for his final shots. Netted 40 FA Cup goals. European Footballer of the Year in 1964. Scored a total 217 League goals.

GREAVSIE ASSESSMENT: `One of my favourite footballers of all time. He was extrovert, flamboyant and spectacular, and never ever dull. An entertainer extraordinary, he had the sharpest reflexes of any player I've seen, and could make a goal out of nothing. Denis had an uncanny ability to hover in the air when heading the ball, and was a master at the overhead bicycle kick. A pussycat off the pitch, he had a fiery temperament on it and was a fierce competitor. If he were at his peak today the transfer bidding would have to start at £50 million.

His amazing record of 40 FA Cup goals did not include the six he netted for Manchester City against Luton in an abandoned tie in 1961. Exactly the same thing happened to him in a youth match.

He was quite rightly known as The King of Old Trafford, long before Eric Cantona came along and stole the crown. For me he will always be The King, and there will never be another Denis Law.´

DENIS LAW'S Most Memorable Goal

MATCH: England v. Rest of the World (Fifa) at Wembley

SEASON: 1963 FA Centenary match

`Ferenc Puskas was on the ball inside the England half and going forward towards goal. He neatly beat one defender and shaped to shoot but noticed that I was in a better position and unselfishly played the ball to me. I beat that genius of a goalkeeper Gordon Banks from about twelve yards. I scored many more spectacular goals but this meant so much to me because of the prestige of the match and the wonderful company in which I was playing. Greavsie stole the man of the match honours. He might have had four goals but for the goalkeeping of the great Lev Yashin, and popped up with the winner late in the game.´

> **FACTFILE:** Born Liverpool, July 17 1940
> Died Wishaw, Scotland, October 6 2003
> Career span: 1956-74. Joined Chelsea from school but was homesick for Scotland. Started his professional career with Hibernian. Along with Denis Law, he had a year with Torino before moving to Arsenal for £70,000 in July 1962. Later played for Nottingham Forest, Sunderland, Hibs and Raith Rovers. A Scottish schoolboy international, he played eight times for England, scoring three goals. Scored 136 of his 301 League goals in England.

GREAVSIE ASSESSMENT: `Joe and I started out together on the Chelsea groundstaff and briefly met up again in Italy. He was a sprinter of a centre-forward, with superb close control, who perfected the give-and-go wall pass technique. He had a devastating spell at Arsenal when feeding off the passes of wily George Eastham.

Joe had a thick Scottish accent, and we used to say he should bring an interpreter into the dressing-room with him. He and Denis Law were a handful on and off the pitch in Italy, where they lived the high life. Both were lucky to survive a crash when Joe turned over his high-powered sports car in Turin. The real Italian Job. Billy Wright bought him for Arsenal where he gave his peak performances before injuries started to rob him of a vital yard of pace.

His elder brother, Gerry, was also a fine marksman, who once scored ten goals in a match for St Mirren.´

JOE BAKER'S Most Memorable Goal

MATCH: England v. Northern Ireland at Wembley
SEASON: 1959-60 Home Championship

•It was my first match for England, and I had to take some terrible stick from my clubmates at Hibs for "playing for the enemy." I was meeting most of the England players for the first time, and had only seen a handful play before. The game was into its sixteenth minute when our left-back Tony Allen pumped a long free-kick in my direction. I managed to confuse the Irish defence by deliberately letting the ball drop past me, and then on its first bounce I met it with a full-blooded right foot shot that sent it flashing into the top corner with goalkeeper Harry Gregg well beaten. It was one of three goals I scored for England, and one that I will never forget. •

Joe Baker, England marksman with the Scottish accent

Bobby Tambling, a deadly finisher with his left foot for Chelsea

Greavsie's Greatest: 12. BOBBY TAMBLING

FACTFILE: Born Storrington, Sussex, September 18 1941 Career span: 1958-72. One of the Drake Ducklings at Chelsea, he made his League debut at 17 and overtook Jimmy Greaves as club record scorer with 164 goals in 302 League games. He scored one goal in three England appearances. Later netted 12 goals in a spell with Crystal Palace before moving into player-management in Ireland with Cork Celtic, Waterford, Shamrock and Cork Alberts. He settled down to live in Ireland following his retirement and became manager of his local side Crosshaven.

GREAVSIE ASSESSMENT: `Bobby was a year younger than me, and eventually took my place in the Chelsea attack and also in the record books. When I left Stamford Bridge for Milan he was an obvious successor, and struck up a terrific partnership with Barry Bridges, another of the stars who rolled off the Chelsea youth conveyor belt. Bobby had explosive speed over short distances and a left foot that was a lethal weapon.

He played the game the way he has lived his life, with a gentlemanly, dedicated and wholehearted approach. Whether out on the left or attacking down the middle, he had the speed and control to open the way to goal. He was a credit to Chelsea in particular and to football in general.

His one chance of a major prize with Chelsea came in the 1967 FA Cup final, when I was playing for Spurs. We were 2-0 up and coasting when Bobby popped up with a late goal to give us a scare. That typified his never give up spirit. As always he was sporting in defeat. Bobby was a good bloke.´

BOBBY TAMBLING'S Most Memorable Goal

MATCH: Liverpool v. Chelsea
SEASON: 1965-66. FA Cup third round

`Liverpool were the Cup holders, and they had jolted us with a goal in the first minute. Not the best start to make at Anfield! But we were in top form that day, and a Peter Osgood goal pulled us level. Midway through the second-half we broke from defence with a move involving all our forwards, starting with me out on the left. I played it inside to Terry Venables and then moved with the play into the Liverpool half. George Graham was the last man to play the ball out on the right, and he fired a good, deep cross into the Liverpool penalty area. I jumped and sent a header looping high into the net for a goal that gave us victory. A winner at Fortress Anfield was very satisfying.´

FACTFILE: Born Ashton-under-Lyme, Lancs, December 8 1941 Career span: 1959-75. Will always be remembered as the man who scored an historic hat-trick for England in the 1966 World Cup final. Played for West Ham in their FA Cup (1964) and European Cup Winners' Cup (1965) winning teams. Collected 180 League goals for West Ham and 22 for Stoke before winding down his League career with West Brom. His goals haul for England was 24 in 49 matches. Became player manager of Telford United, and then briefly managed Chelsea. Knighted in 1998.

GREAVSIE ASSESSMENT: `There have been few more effective strikers in an England shirt than Geoff at his peak. He was strong, unselfish, could shield a ball as well as anybody I've seen, and had a hammer in his left foot. He was always positive, both in his attitude and his actions, and his honest endeavour made him a great example to young players. There was also a sophistication in his positional sense and neat, glancing headers that was a hallmark of the stylish West Ham of the 1960s.

He owed a lot to the vision of Hammers manager Ron Greenwood. Geoff will admit that he was a fairly ordinary wing-half until Greenwood spotted his potential as a striker and moved him into a full-time attacking role.

His almost intuitive understanding of the play of West Ham clubmates Bobby Moore and Martin Peters was a key factor in the success of England in 1966. We have remained good friends far beyond our football careers.´

GEOFF HURST'S Most Memorable Goal
MATCH: England v. Argentina
SEASON: 1966 World Cup quarter-final

•It was a made-in-West-Ham goal. Martin Peters floated a centre from the left in front of the Argentine defenders. It was a move we had perfected as clubmates at Upton Park, and here it was being presented in my World Cup debut. While the ball was on its way into the penalty area I made ground towards the near post and arrived at just the right time to be able to direct it into the net with a glancing header. The goal put us through to the World Cup semi-finals. Obviously my hat-trick in the final was special and changed my entire life, but that goal against Argentina gave me the confidence to believe that I belonged on the World Cup stage.•

Artist Art Turner's impression of Geoff Hurst hammering his World Cup hat-trick goal

Jeff Astle, a throwback to the old-style centre-forwards

FACTFILE: Born Eastwood, Notts, May 13 1942
Died: Burton-upon-Trent, January 19 2002
Career span: 1959-75. Scored 31 goals in 96 League games
for Notts County before joining West Brom in 1964. Capped
five times by England, he won an FA Cup winners' medal with
West Brom in 1968 and was in their League Cup-winning team
in 1966, and was a runner-up with them in 1967 and 1970.
He scored 137 League goals for West Brom, and played out
his career in non-League football after a season with
Hellenic FC in South Africa.

GREAVSIE ASSESSMENT: `Jeff was a throwback to the old-style centre-forwards who put emphasis on the physical aspect of the game. His aggressive style showed that he had come under the influence of Tommy Lawton early in his career at Notts County. He was magnificent in the air, and scored many spectacular goals with bullet headers. An entertaining character both on and off the pitch, Jeff's brief England career was clouded by his missing of an open goal when he came on as a substitute against Brazil in the 1970 World Cup finals. He deserved to be remembered for his goals rather than his misses.

His fame later transcended football because of his singing and joking appearances on the Skinner and Baddiel Fantasy Football TV show. Then, tragically, his physical style of play caught up with him when he reached middle-age. Jeff suffered degenerative brain disease and died at the age of 59. A verdict of death by industrial injury was recorded at his inquest. It is the price many former pros have suffered for heading those old leather footballs.´

JEFF ASTLE'S Most Memorable Goal

MATCH: West Bromwich Albion v. Everton at Wembley
SEASON: 1968 FA Cup final

❛The goal that meant most to me has to be the one that won the FA Cup for West Brom against Everton. I got possession near the halfway line, avoided a tackle during a run of 20 yards and then tried a long-range shot. The ball hit centre-half Brian Labone, and as it rebounded back into my path I caught it on the volley and watched it fly from my left foot into the top corner of the net. Everton had been hot favourites, but the goal rocked them back on their heels and you could almost see the confidence draining out of them. We went potty at the final whistle, and I will never forget the look on Alan Ball's face. He had tears in his eyes and looked as if he had been mugged.❜

Greavsie's Greatest: 15. MARTIN PETERS

FACTFILE: Born Plaistow, November 8 1943
Career span: 1962-80. Stole through defences to plunder 169 League goals with West Ham (70), Tottenham (46) and Norwich City (44) before joining Sheffield United as player-coach, taking over as team manager for a brief spell in January 1981. He was a member of the West Ham team that won the 1965 European Cup Winners' Cup, and he was a winner with Tottenham in two League Cup finals and a Uefa Cup final. Capped 67 times by England, he scored 21 goals including the second one in the 1966 World Cup final.

GREAVSIE ASSESSMENT: `We both learnt our football on the playing fields of Dagenham, and our careers overlapped when I made up the weight in the £220,000 transfer deal that took Martin to Spurs and me to West Ham in 1970. The move worked out much better for Martin than for me, and he became enormously popular at White Hart Lane.

Martin was a superbly gifted artist, tip-toeing through defences as the Gentle Executioner. Alf Ramsey once described him as a player ten years ahead of his time. He was never really completely appreciated by the majority of fans, but ask any pro and they will tell you he was class from head to toe.

His positional play was masterly, and his glancing headers – particularly at the near post – caught many goalkeepers napping. Martin is one of the few midfield players featured in my top 50 list simply because his main role was the making and taking of goals. Without Martin, Ramsey may not have discovered his Wingless Wonders.´

MARTIN PETERS' Most Memorable Goal

MATCH: England v. West Germany at Wembley
SEASON: 1966 World Cup final

`It was probably one of the simplest goals I ever scored, but the memory of it will remain with me for always. German defender Wolfgang Weber blocked a shot from my West Ham team-mate Geoff Hurst, and as the ball dropped I hit it right-footed on the volley into the back of the net from about six yards. There were just twelve minutes to go, and the goal gave England a 2-1 lead. I thought I had scored the winning goal, but the Germans equalised in the last minute – and the rest is history. In extra-time Geoff went on to complete his great hat-trick, and our lives were from then on never quite the same again.`

Martin Peters, the gentle executioner who was ten years ahead of his time

Francis Lee, who was a main man at Maine Road

FACTFILE: Born Westhoughton, Lancs, April 29 1944
Made his Bolton debut at 16 and scored 92 League goals
before joining Manchester City for £65,000 in 1965. City's
leading marksman for five consecutive years from 1969-70,
and the League's top scorer in 1971-72 with 33 goals,
including a club record 13 penalties. Collected League
championship medal (1968), FA Cup (1969), League Cup and
European Cup Winners' Cup (1970) medals with City. Won a
second League title with Derby in 1975, taking his League
goals haul to 229. Ten goals in 27 England games.

GREAVSIE ASSESSMENT: `Franny was a good businessman off the pitch and an expert at the goalscoring business. He could play wide on the right or as a central striker, and his willingness to run at defences made him a difficult man to mark out of a match. Franny was always cheerful and bouncing with confidence, and this attitude spilled over into his game. He had a low centre of gravity, good close control and packed a stunning right-foot shot.

He could also look after himself as he proved when having a toe-to-toe punch-up with Norman Hunter when both were ordered off at Derby after 'Bites Yer Legs' had accused Franny of diving for a penalty. Franny's penalty area antics earned him the fitting nickname Lee Won Pen.

Using money made from his extensive wastepaper business, he bought Man City when the club was at Maine Road before it became the mega-rich outfit it is today. He also had a spell as a racehorse owner and trainer. Some life.´

FRANCIS LEE'S Most Memorable Goal

MATCH: Newcastle United v. Manchester City
SEASON: 1967-68, First Division

•It was a game we had to win to clinch the League championship. We were clinging on to a 3-2 lead when Colin Bell put me away through the middle with a superb pass. I skipped past two defenders and then clipped the ball wide of the oncoming goalkeeper. Newcastle fought back to make it 4-3, but we held out to win a pulsating match and the title. I scored a more spectacular goal for Derby in their League championship season, but the reason I remember the City goal at Newcastle so well is that it brought me my first major honour in football. It helped lift the Blues out of the red shadow being cast from Old Trafford.•

> **FACTFILE:** Born Hatfield, Herts, October 11 1944
> Career span: 1963-77. Took his considerable skills to the
> United States after amassing 169 League goals with Fulham
> (27 in two spells), QPR (106) and Manchester City (36).
> Was top marksman for QPR in 1966-67, when they won the
> League Cup and Third Division championship, and again the
> following season when they gained promotion to the First
> Division. Capped nine times by England. He had three
> spells playing for Tampa Bay Rowdies, and also managed
> them from 1984 to 1986 and was chief executive.

GREAVSIE ASSESSMENT: `A "now you see me, now you don't" magician with the ball at his feet, Rodney was one of the most creative forces in English football during his eventful career. The fans loved him, but quite a few coaches tended to resent him because of his refusal to conform to their rigid plans. He was a one-off original, who believed in doing things his way. Had he been born in South America they would no doubt have built a statue in his honour but his individuality was not always appreciated in England.

He sometimes infuriated his own team-mates with his clowning, but he was never ever dull. When he joined Francis Lee, Mike Summerbee and Colin Bell at Manchester City it looked like a dream signing. But Rodney's ball-holding style of play interrupted the City flow and he carried the can for costing them the championship. He teamed-up with George Best in a Sunshine Boys finish to their careers at Fulham. On a good day, they were simply irresistible.

RODNEY MARSH'S Most Memorable Goal
MATCH: Queens Park Rangers v. West Bromwich Albion at Wembley
SEASON: 1967 League Cup final

•We were trailing 2-0 at half-time but hit back to win 3-2. I recall our manager Alec Stock saying to me at half-time, 'Rodney, nobody in their team is fit to lace your boots. Go out there and show them what football, real football, is all about. Go out and prove to the world you are the greatest.' Alec's words worked because I felt ten feet tall in the second-half and I scored a goal I'll never forget. I took the ball on a zig-zag run from the halfway line, wrong-footing three West Brom defenders and then sending a low right-foot shot into the net. That made it 2-2, and from then on West Brom weren't in with a hope. It was a goal I'd always dreamt of scoring since I was a kid.•

Rodney Marsh, a "now you see me, now you don't" magician with the ball at his feet

Martin Chivers, a gliding, gentle giant of the game

FACTFILE: Born Southampton April 27 1945
Scored 96 goals in 175 League games for his hometown
club Southampton before joining Tottenham in January 1968
for a then British record £125,000. While with Spurs he
won 24 England caps (13 goals), two League Cup winners'
medals and played in the winning Uefa Cup final team
against Wolves (1972). Collected 118 League goals in 278
games with Spurs and then became a 33-goal marksman with
Swiss club Servette. Later played briefly for Norwich and
Brighton before going into non-League football.

GREAVSIE ASSESSMENT: `For a man with such a massive frame, Martin was surprisingly nimble, and he glided along the ground with a lazy-looking stride that was deceptively quick. We had a brief partnership at the back-end of my career with Spurs, and I got to appreciate his mixture of power and finesse, which was shown off to better effect when he played alongside the crafty Alan Gilzean. He had the character to make a comeback after a knee injury that threatened to wreck his career. If anything, he was an even more accomplished player after his lay-off, because he added a physical edge to his game that had previously been more about speed and subtlety.

Southampton fans would argue that he was at his most dynamic when partnering young Mike Channon in the early stages of their careers at The Dell. An intelligent, well-educated man, I was surprised he did not have a crack at League club management.´

MARTIN CHIVERS' Most Memorable Goal
MATCH: Stoke City v. Tottenham
SEASON: 1970-71, First Division

•I have good memories of the Uefa Cup victory when I scored a couple of crackers at Wolves in the first-leg of the final, but the goal that has stuck in my memory came at Stoke. I collected the ball out on the left touchline under pressure from that formidable Stoke defender Denis Smith. As he made his challenge, I shouldered him off and managed to keep possession. Then I set off for goal and Gordon Banks came off his line to narrow the angle. I checked, changed feet and bent the ball round Gordon and into the far corner of the goal. I really enjoyed that one, particularly as it was against one of the all-time great goalkeepers in Banksie.•

FACTFILE: Born Orcheston, Wiltshire, October 28 1948
Career span: 1966-86. Progressed from village-team foot-
ball to First Division fame after being spotted playing on
Salisbury Plain. Kicked off his career with Southampton
aged 16 and in two spells there scored a club record 185
League goals. Sandwiched in between were 24 goals in 72
League matches for Manchester City. Netted 21 goals in 44
England appearances. Played briefly for Newcastle, Bristol
Rovers, Norwich and Portsmouth, and played frequently in
South Africa before turning to racehorse training.

GREAVSIE ASSESSMENT: `A quick, well-balanced player, Mike was one of the most dangerous strikers in the 'old' First Division when in possession and running at defences at top speed. He had good close control, finished well with his right foot and had excellent positional sense. He was expert at deceiving defenders with a sudden change of pace, and used to announce his goals with a trademark windmilling of his right arm. Mike would, I'm sure, have won many more England caps but for his loyalty to Saints when they were locked in the Second Division. He played a key role in helping them win the FA Cup with a stunning victory over Manchester United at Wembley in 1976.

He has since become a leading trainer of racehorses who, like Mike, are thoroughbreds. Showing the character that always shone through on the football pitch, he has battled back from horrendous injuries received in a 2008 motorway car crash.´

MIKE CHANNON'S Most Memorable Goal
MATCH: Southampton v. Coventry City
SEASON: 1971-72, First Division

'The goal I remember above all others was during my first spell at Southampton. I collected the ball back in our own penalty area and started running with it. Everybody – including me – was waiting for me to pass. The goal seemed an awful long way away and it was in my mind to off-load the ball to somebody nearer the Coventry penalty area. But their defence opened up invitingly and so I thought I would keep on going. Suddenly I thought 'Blimey, a goal's on here' and so I gathered speed, a bit like a racehorse entering the final couple of furlongs. I got to the edge of the box and let fly with a right-foot shot that arrowed into the net. I was happily knackered.'

Art Turner
2010

Mike Channon, a thoroughbred of a footballer who now trains thoroughbreds

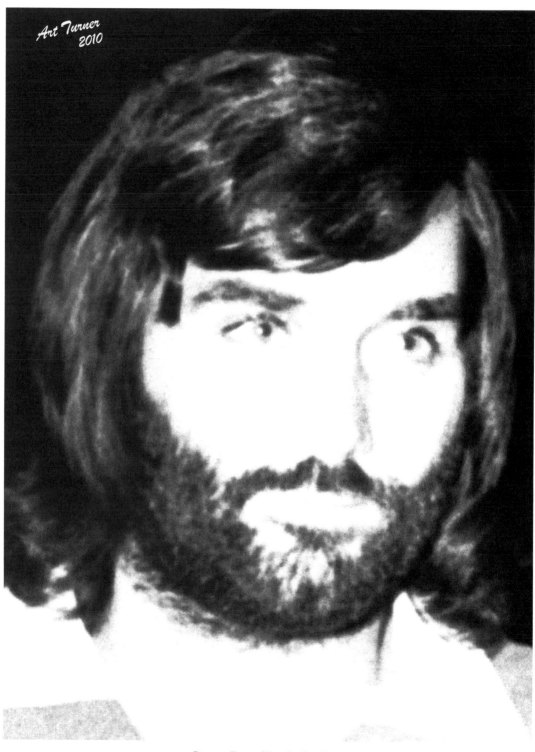

George Best, Simply the Best

Greavsie's Greatest: 20. GEORGE BEST

FACTFILE: Born Belfast, May 22 1946
Died London, November 25 2005
Career span: 1963-1983. Scored 137 goals in 361 League
games for Man United, won two League championship medals.
In 1968 won a European Cup winners' medal and was voted FWA
and European Footballer of the Year. Retired in 1973, but
came back to play for a string of clubs including Stockport
County, Cork Celtic, LA Aztecs, Fulham, Hibs, San José
Earthquakes, Fort Lauderdale Strikers, Bournemouth and
Brisbane Lions. Total League goals: 205 in 579 games.

GREAVSIE ASSESSMENT: `I have no hesitation in saying that George was the greatest British footballer of my lifetime, and probably anybody else's lifetime. At his peak with Man United, he was a phenomenal player with perfect balance, total control of the ball even when at top speed, was as brave as a lion and could conjure his way past defenders in confined space.

Most of his goals were memorable. He didn't just decorate matches. He decided them. It makes me angry when I see people write or say that he wasted his talent with his off-the-field lifestyle. He played more than 600 matches in all competitions and scored over 250 goals. How is that wasting his talent? Would he have been a better player had he not liked the birds and the booze so much? Who knows. Perhaps he would have lost his edge had he lived a Bobby Charlton-style life. Each to his own. George and I were good pals, so I am biased, but for me he really was *Simply the Best.´*

GEORGE BEST'S Most Memorable Goal
MATCH: Manchester United v. Tottenham
SEASON: 1970-71, First Division

•There was one I scored in the States when I managed to run the ball around seven defenders before scoring, but the goal that gave me greatest satisfaction was against my dear friend and finest of all goalkeepers, Pat Jennings. Pat came out to make a punched clearance and the ball fell to me on the left-hand side of the penalty box. There were so many players between the goal and me that I decided to lob it over Pat's head before he could regain his composure. There was a Spurs defender covering behind Pat on the goal-line, but I managed to squeeze the ball into the net with about an inch and a quarter to spare! Pat was sporting enough to say, "Great goal, you bastard."•

```
FACTFILE: Shortheath, Staffs, July 31 1946
Career span: 1963-80. Played for Walsall, Fulham, Leicester
and Leeds before becoming Barnsley player-manager. Scored
110 First Division goals for Leeds in 273 matches, won
a League championship medal (1974), and winners' medals
in the FA Cup (1972), and Fairs Cup (1971). European Cup
finalist in 1975. A runner-up in three FA Cup finals. His
total League goals: 224. Scored 10 goals for England in
19 games. Briefly managed Leeds, and was later in charge
at Scunthorpe, back to Barnsley and then Lincoln City.
```

GREAVSIE ASSESSMENT: `There have been few sharper players in the box in post-war football. Allan was nicknamed 'Sniffer' because of his knack for sniffing out the half chance. Once he had got the scent he rarely missed. He had the killer instinct in front of goal, could score with either foot, headed with accuracy and was a master at creating space for himself in the crowded penalty area. I first became aware of him when he was with Fulham, and my mate Johnny Haynes told me he was a natural goalscorer.

Clarkie, the second of five brothers to play professional football, also had a lot of bottle. He made his international debut for England in the 1970 World Cup final group match against Czechoslovakia in Mexico. Alf Ramsey called for a volunteer to take any penalty, and it was Sniffer who put his hand up. Sure enough, England got a penalty and the ice-cool Clarke put it away to earn England a place in the quarter-finals.´

ALLAN CLARKE'S Most Memorable Goal
MATCH: Leeds United v. Arsenal at Wembley
SEASON: 1972 FA Cup final

`This was the Centenary FA Cup final and so the build up was even more intense than usual. Arsenal had won the Double the year before and were defending the trophy. The game was goalless and about seven minutes into the second-half, when Mick Jones made a fast run down our right side. He got past full-back Bob McNab and drove the ball hard into the box at about hip height. I was motoring through to try to get on the end of it and my first reaction was to volley the ball, but it suddenly started to dip and so I instinctively threw myself forward and made a diving header into the bottom corner of the net. I scored a lot better goals, but this one was extra-special for me.´

Art Turner
2010

Allan Clarke, who sniffed out scores of goals

Peter Osgood, who swerved and glided past defenders as if on a magic carpet

FACTFILE: Born Windsor, February 20 1947
Died Slough, Berks, March 1 2006
Career span: 1964-79. Started and ended his career with
Chelsea, scoring 105 League goals in 280 games. He also
gathered 28 League goals in 126 matches for Southampton
and helped them win the FA Cup in 1976. He won an FA Cup
winners' medal with Chelsea in 1970 (scoring in every
round), and the following season was the star of Chelsea's
European Cup Winners' Cup-winning team. Had brief spells
with Norwich and in the USA. Won four England caps.

GREAVSIE ASSESSMENT: `One of the most naturally gifted footballers of my lifetime, Peter had the sort of skills that should have earned him dozens of England caps and world-wide fame. But he lacked total dedication and application. We shared the same birthday and both of us started our careers at Stamford Bridge. He graced the Bridge with his diamond-studded skills and memorable goals. What a pity he never reached his full exciting potential.

He had the character to overcome the cruel blow of a broken leg early in his career, but was never able to shake off a seemingly casual approach to the game. Peter could swerve and glide past defenders as if on a magic carpet, and gave beautifully weighted passes. If he had been able and willing to give just a little more of himself to football, he would have become one of the all-time greats. How sad that he was taken from us so early. He was a unique and lovable character, a true one-off.´

PETER OSGOOD'S Most Memorable Goal

MATCH: Burnley v. Chelsea
SEASON: 1966-67, First Division

`The ball was cleared to me and there was nobody to pass to, so I started off on a run. I was about ten yards inside our own half when I set off, and everywhere I looked there were claret and blue shirts of Burnley defenders. Three of them tried to tackle me, and I dummied and feinted past them one after the other. Then goalkeeper Adam Blacklaw came off his line at me, but I saw a gap and drove the ball low into the net with my left foot. Even the Burnley fans stood up and applauded! Another special goal in my memory was my diving header from a Charlie Cooke cross in the 1970 FA Cup final replay at Old Trafford when Chelsea beat Leeds 2-1.´

FACTFILE: Dundee, December 14 1947
Career span: 1963-79. Played his first match for Leeds at the age of 15 and his last at 39. In between two spells at Elland Road he had a season with York City and spent three years in the North American Soccer League. In 676 appearances for Leeds he scored a club record 238 goals. Won two League championship medals, an FA Cup winners' medal and a European Cup runners-up medal. He netted four goals in 21 internationals for Scotland, including a goal against Zaire at the 1974 World Cup finals.

GREAVSIE ASSESSMENT: `Peter packed one of the hardest shots I have ever seen. Goalkeepers knew they had to be alert the moment he settled on the ball because he could score from prodigious distances. He came from my school of not being very effective in the air, and he used his left leg for standing on. But his rifle shooting with his right foot made him one of the most feared and respected strikers of any era and earned him the fitting nickname of 'Hot Shot' Lorimer.

He was a key finisher in that outstanding Leeds United team of the Don Revie era, which was famed and feared not only for its skilled football but also the muscle provided by the likes of Billy Bremner, big Jack Charlton and Norman 'Bites Yer Legs' Hunter. Peter has stayed in close contact with Leeds through his local radio broadcasting and newspaper columns, and has served on the United board, a great servant of the club where he is a legend.´

PETER LORIMER'S Most Memorable Goal
MATCH: Leeds United v. Manchester City
SEASON: 1971-72, First Division

⁶I was thirty yards out from goal when I gathered a long ball from Billy Bremner. I tried to lob it over a City defender, but it was deflected in a slow arc over my left shoulder. As it dropped I connected on the volley and the ball flashed into the net. A goal that most people remember me scoring was disallowed. It happened in the last moments of a 1967 FA Cup semi-final against Chelsea when Johnny Giles tapped a free-kick to me and I let fire with the right peg. It flew through the Chelsea defensive wall and beat 'keeper Peter Bonetti all ends up. There was pandemonium when the referee ruled the equaliser out for what seemed no reason.⁹

Peter Lorimer, the Hot Shot of Leeds and Scotland

Frank Worthington, who treated the football pitch as his personal stage

FACTFILE: Born Halifax, November 23 1948
Career span: 1966-88. One of three brothers to play League football, he began his career with Huddersfield Town in 1966 before playing for Leicester City, Bolton, Birmingham City, Leeds United, Sunderland, Southampton, Brighton, Tranmere Rovers, Preston, Stockport County and Galway United. Played into his 40s, making 757 League appearances and scoring 234 goals. He also played extensively in the North American Soccer League, South Africa, Sweden and in English non-League football. Won eight England caps.

GREAVSIE ASSESSMENT: `The football field was always like a stage for Frank, who never failed to give fans value for money. His highly individual style did not meet with the approval of coaches, but he was always worth watching. What a pity high blood pressure stopped him signing for Liverpool in the early 1970s. I think he would have become a new king of the Kop in that outstanding Liverpool team that Bill Shankly built. He had marvellous dribbling skills, and he could unlock a safe door with his left foot.

As with George Best, he liked the ladies and led a playboy lifestyle; and as with George Best, Frank did things his way on and off the pitch. He became a have-boots-will-travel globetrotting footballer after laying the foundations to his career with Huddersfield, Leicester and Bolton. He was player-manager at Tranmere, when I am sure he would have told his players: "Don't do as I do, do as I say." What an entertainer, what a character.´

FRANK WORTHINGTON'S Most Memorable Goal

MATCH: Bolton v Ipswich Town
SEASON: 1978-79, First Division

•There was a Bolton throw-in 15 yards from the Ipswich left corner flag. The ball was flicked on to me in a central position by Alan Gowling. I had my back to the goal as I controlled the ball with my head and glanced it down on to my left foot. Then I juggled with it while moving away from the Ipswich goal as three defenders converged on me. Suddenly, and quite instinctively, I flicked the ball over my head and turned to face the goal as it dropped. As I wheeled round I connected on the volley with my left foot and sent it wide of diving goalkeeper Paul Cooper and into the right-hand stanchion. Magic! It was replayed on ITV's football show opening titles for months.•

FACTFILE: Born Liverpool, April 8 1949
Career span: 1966-82. Made his League debut for Everton at
the age of 16 and totalled 102 goals for the Merseysiders
in 231 League matches. Won a League championship medal
in 1969-70. Joined Manchester City for £200,000 in 1974,
and later played for Bristol City, Hereford and Norwich
City. Scored two goals in six England appearances. After
hanging up his boots in 1982, he travelled the managerial
roundabout with Oldham (twice), Everton, Manchester City
and Ipswich Town.

GREAVSIE ASSESSMENT: `Manager Harry Catterick got attacked by Everton fans furious that he had picked unknown kid Joe in place of Goodison legend Alex Young, but he gradually won over the supporters with his powerful and direct style of play. He was a tall, well-built centre-forward with old school habits that made him suitable for the No 9 Everton shirt that had been worn by icons Dixie Dean and Tommy Lawton.

Strong in the air and quick on the ground, he would have won many more than his six England caps but for a recurring back injury. It was finally a knee injury that forced him to quit playing in 1982 after he had been voted Norwich City's player of the year. He was a positive manager, but not the luckiest. He twice steered Oldham to the FA Cup semi-finals, each time going down to Man United in replays. Joe has always been a good advert for our game. I picked him just ahead of Goodison great Bob Latchford in my Top 50.´

JOE ROYLE'S Most Memorable Goal

MATCH: Leeds United v. Everton
SEASON: 1969-70, First Division

•It was the season Leeds were chasing the treble, and they were our closest rivals in the chance for the League championship. We had been under the cosh when Alan Ball got possession of the ball for us out on the right. Ballie looked up to see me making ground from the opposite side of the box. He expertly dropped the ball in at the near post, and I guided it into the net with my head before goalkeeper Gary Sprake even realised I was around. We went on to win the championship, with Leeds runners-up. Back then there was nothing quite as satisfying as scoring against Leeds when they were Don Revie's mean machine.•

Joe Royle, powerful and direct centre-forward in the old school style

Brian Kidd, who will never forget his nineteenth birthday in 1968

FACTFILE: Born Manchester, May 29 1949
Career span: 1967-84. Consistently harvested goals with
Man United (52), Arsenal (30), Man City (44), Everton
(11) and Bolton (14) before invading the USA: Atlanta
Chiefs (23 goals), Fort Lauderdale Strikers (34 goals)
and Minnesota Strikers (8). Hit the headlines when scoring
for Man United in the 1968 European Cup final on his 19th
birthday. Scored one goal in two England appearances. Has
been assistant manager at both Old Trafford and Eastlands,
and has been the boss at Preston and Blackburn.

GREAVSIE ASSESSMENT: `One of the most exciting teenage prospects I have ever seen, Brian didn't quite live up to his early promise. I thought he was going to win a cupboardful of England caps but he was rewarded with only two by Alf Ramsey in the build-up to the 1970 World Cup finals.

He was at his best in his early days with United, when he played with a persistence and pace that drove defences into nervous breakdowns, particularly when he had masters like Best, Law and Charlton backing him up.

His managerial career has been a reflection of his playing days, better in support as a number two rather than holding the reins as manager. He was productive as right-hand man to Alex Ferguson at Old Trafford and eventually returned to Manchester City where he became assistant to Roberto Mancini.

Brian has had a career of which to be proud, but he must know in his heart that it could have been so much better.´

BRIAN KIDD'S Most Memorable Goal

MATCH: Manchester United v. Benfica at Wembley
SEASON: 1968 European Cup final

•I remember this match and my goal as much for the emotion of the occasion as anything else. We were beating Benfica 2-1 with the game into extra-time when I had a header pushed on to the bar by Benfica goalkeeper Henrique. I threw myself forward and got my head to the rebound to send the ball into the net. Bobby Charlton wrapped it all up when he added a fourth goal and his second from my centre. There has never been a night like it to match the emotion, and there were tears everywhere you looked. We all cuddled Sir Matt Busby, who with Bobby had survived the Munich air crash ten years earlier. What a birthday that was for me!•

> **FACTFILE:** Born Fulham January 7 1950
> Career span: 1968-79. Started as a full-back with non-League Tonbridge, then converted to centre-forward with Fulham. Moved to Luton in July 1969 and was then bought by Newcastle for £186,000 in 1971. Gathered 95 League goals for Newcastle in 187 matches before moving to Arsenal for £333,000 in 1976. Recurring injuries forced his retirement at 28. His total goals haul was 191 in 372 League games. Highlight of his 14 England caps was all five goals against Cyprus in April 1975.

GREAVSIE ASSESSMENT: `The 'Tiger of Tyneside', he had his greatest moments with Newcastle, where he remains an idol in the Jackie Milburn mould. His two greatest assets before injuries took their toll were his sprinter's speed and his bomb of a left foot that smashed in goals from all distances and angles.

He was not one to keep his opinions to himself, and shot from the lip to an extent where he used to put pressure on himself and his team-mates. I remember in particular him talking a good match before the 1974 FA Cup final against Liverpool, but then failed to put action where his mouth was when it came to the game. All he managed to do was motivate Liverpool.

Supermac was a great-hearted competitor who always gave the fans full value for money, and don't forget that he collected his goals in an era when the emphasis was heavily on defence.´

MALCOLM MACDONALD'S Most Memorable Goal

MATCH: Newcastle United v. Leicester City
SEASON: 1976-77, First Division

‘Irving Nattrass took the ball at top speed on a break from the Newcastle penalty area after a period of heavy Leicester pressure. He released a square pass into my path when I was about 40 yards from goal. I struck the ball first time with my left foot and had the satisfaction of seeing it still on the rise as it hit the back of the Leicester net. It was the sort of goal you could not have rehearsed in training. It was pure, off-the-cuff perfection. The reason it is so memorable for me is that it's the only goal of the 260 or so that I scored that made the hair on the back of my neck stand up. By the way, Irving should have won at least 50 England caps. A versatile and hugely underrated foobtaller who deserves recognition.’

Malcolm Macdonald, Supermac and Supermouth

John Toshack, a master marksman and well-travelled manager

```
FACTFILE: Born Cardiff March 22 1949
Career span: 1965-84. Scored 74 goals in 161 League games
for Cardiff and then  had an almost identical striking rate
with Liverpool: 74 goals in 172 First Division matches.
While at Anfield he collected three League championship
medals, and an FA Cup and two Uefa Cup winners medals.
Netted 12 goals in 40 games for Wales. Became Swansea
player-manager in 1978 and steered them to the First
Division in 1980-81. Had two spells managing Wales between
management in Portugal, Spain, Turkey, Italy and France.
```

GREAVSIE ASSESSMENT: `His partnership with Kevin Keegan was one of the great club combinations of the 1970s. John was a constructive and creative target man, continually bringing Keegan into the action with neat lay-offs, particularly with his head. He had good positional instinct, and could apply a powerful and accurate finishing touch. Only injuries prevented him sharing in Liverpool's European Cup triumphs with Bob Paisley's Red dream machine. An intelligent man with good tactical knowledge, he was in demand on the managerial circuit after guiding Swansea City to promotion to the old First Division as a thoughtful player-manager.

Tosh never ducks a challenge and has managed Real Madrid twice, Real Sociedad twice as well as being involved in club management in Portugal, Turkey, Italy and France. He was never able to lift Wales out of a rut of mediocrity in two spells as international manager.´

JOHN TOSHACK'S Most Memorable Goal
MATCH: Barcelona v. Liverpool
SEASON: 1975-76, Uefa Cup semi-final 1st leg

•Goalkeeper Ray Clemence kicked a long ball out of his hands and I flicked it on to Kevin Keegan, who supplied me with an instant return pass as I moved towards the Barcelona penalty area. The moment the ball came back to me from Kevin I steered it into the net for the only goal of the match. It was as simple as that. No coach could have planned it. I think it was the simplicity of it all that gave me so much satisfaction. I scored more spectacular goals, but this one had a certain style about it that meant the goal remained in my memory as a reminder of just how straightforward and uncomplicated the game can be.•

FACTFILE: Born Islington, October 10 1950
Career span: 1968-83. Became an Arsenal apprentice after being discovered by goalkeeper Bob Wilson while coaching local schools. Recovered from a broken ankle to score the Wembley goal against Liverpool that clinched the League and Cup double in 1970-71. Scored 31 League goals for Arsenal in 133 matches, then 34 goals in 106 League games for Derby. Also played for Nottingham Forest, Southampton and in the USA and Hong Kong. Capped once by England, Don Revie playing him out of position on the left-wing.

GREAVSIE ASSESSMENT: `Charlie, the local hero who came off the terraces to play for Arsenal, would have established himself as one of the great modern strikers but for a succession of injuries. There was an iconic moment when young Charlie lay flat on his back after scoring the extra-time goal that sunk Liverpool and clinched the Double for the Gunners in 1971. He was a non-conformist who refused to be cramped by instruction, and he had many fall outs with Bertie Mee and the coaching staff before moving to Derby County. I always thought that Cockney Charlie was like a fish out of water at the Baseball Ground but he settled down to score more goals for the Rams than he did for the Gunners.

The saying 'Football died the day Charlie George got a bubble perm' shows the impact he made as a long-haired icon of the Seventies. He had prodigious skill and the gift of being able to strike the ball with a minimum of backlift but maximum power. These days he's back 'home' at Arsenal as an Emirates Stadium tour guide. He should never have left.´

CHARLIE GEORGE'S Most Memorable Goal

MATCH: Derby County v. Real Madrid
SEASON: 1975-76, European Cup

'There was a flowing movement early in the game, with Colin Todd and Archie Gemmill swinging the ball from one side of the pitch to the other. I moved with the play into Real's 18-yard box and, as I arrived, Archie found me with a perfect pass. All in one movement I struck a fierce left-foot volley into the far right corner of the net. It was one of four goals I scored in the two legs, including a hat-trick in the home leg at the Baseball Ground. That's the good news. The bad news is that we lost 6-5 on aggregate. The other most memorable goal was when I scored for Arsenal against Liverpool in the 1970 FA Cup final. Arsenal fans still ask me about that one today.'

Charlie George, the local hero who came off the terraces to play for Arsenal

Art Turner
2010

Kevin Keegan, European Footballer of the Year in back-to-back seasons

Greavsie's Greatest: 30. KEVIN KEEGAN

FACTFILE: Born Armthorpe, Yorkshire, February 14 1951
Career span: 1968-84. Joined Liverpool from Scunthorpe for
£35,000 in 1971. Scored two goals in the 1974 FA Cup final
win against Newcastle, and won three championship medals
and the European Cup in 1977 before a £500,000 transfer
to Hamburg where he won back-to-back European Footballer
of the Year awards. Netted 21 goals in 63 England games.
Returned to English football with Southampton and then
Newcastle. Later managed Newcastle twice, had 20 months
in charge of England and managed Fulham and Man City.

GREAVSIE ASSESSMENT: `I always admired Kevin's great industry. There were more skilful and more inventive players, but his remarkable workrate when coupled with his considerable ability lifted him above most of his rivals. The way he turned himself into a world-class player by sheer effort is a lesson to every young professional in the game.

England were unlucky that both he and his creative partner from West Ham, Trevor Brooking, were injured during the 1982 World Cup campaign, otherwise Ron Greenwood's team might have made more of an impressive impact.

Kevin has made even bigger headlines as an outspoken and occasionally temperamental manager who has always been willing to put the emphasis on attacking play. His various teams always seem to reflect his approach to playing – bright, industrious, competitive and with quite a lot of flair.´

KEVIN KEEGAN'S Most Memorable Goal
MATCH: England v. Italy at Wembley
SEASON: 1977 World Cup qualifying match

˙My old mate Trevor Brooking fired a beautifully flighted cross deep into the Italian penalty area. I raced towards the near post to meet it with my head and sent the ball wide of goalkeeper Dino Zoff inside the far post. I was able to return the compliment later in the game when my through ball let Trevor in for his first England goal. Trevor and I always brought the best out of each other and we knew where to be to make the most of each other's possession. The biggest choker for the pair of us is that we were carrying injuries going into the 1982 World Cup finals, and all we managed between us was late substitute appearances in the last game.˙

FACTFILE: Born Glasgow March 4 1951
Career span: 1969-89. Scored 112 goals in 204 League games for Celtic, then 118 goals in 355 League matches for Liverpool. Scotland's top marksman with 30 goals in 102 games. Won everything in sight in Scotland and collected seven English League titles, three European Cups and five domestic cups. Became player-manager of Liverpool in 1985 and guided them to three League wins and two FA Cups from 1985-1991. Steered Blackburn to the Premier League title but had no success in charge at Newcastle and Celtic.

GREAVSIE ASSESSMENT: `Kenny was arguably the greatest British striker of his generation, shooting himself to legend status. He was always composed and controlled in the penalty area, no matter how great the pressure and he was continually a thought and a deed ahead of most defenders. His finishing was mercilessly accurate, and he played without fuss or unnecessary theatrics.

Liverpool fans were plunged into mourning when Kevin Keegan was allowed to move to Hamburg – not realising that, in Kenny, manager Bob Paisley had got a superior player. He quickly became the King of the Kop and, in harness with Ian Rush, was the main motivator of the team that ruled European football in the 1980s. The sympathetic way he behaved in the wake of the Hillsbrough disaster showed he is a man of great character.

His lifting of the Premier League title with Blackburn proved that he was a manager of exceptional judgement.´

KENNY DALGLISH'S Most Memorable Goal
MATCH: Liverpool v. Bruges at Wembley
SEASON: 1978 European Cup final

•I'm sorry but I cannot be pinned down on this. I considered every goal I scored memorable in its own way. The only thing that mattered was the ball crossing the goal-line. In terms of satisfaction, my goal that settled the 1978 European Cup final against Bruges at Wembley took some beating. I was in possession deep in the Bruges penalty area, and waited for the goalkeeper to commit himself and then chipped the ball over him and into the net. The momentum of my run took me over the hoardings behind the goal and I looked up to see the Liverpool fans going wild. From that moment on I was totally accepted by them. It was a great way to finish my first season at Anfield.•

Kenny Dalglish, scored a century of goals in Scotland and England

Mind the gap, it's Joe Jordan!

FACTFILE: Born Cleland, Scotland December 15 1951
Career span: 1968-88. Playing for Greenock Morton while
finishing his apprenticeship as a draughtsman, Joe was
snapped up by Leeds after just eight Scottish League
matches. Scored 35 goals in 170 League games with Leeds,
winning a League championship medal in 1973-74. Joined Man
United for £350,000 in 1978. Scored 37 goals in 109 League
matches for United, then played for AC Milan and Hellas
Verona before returning to England with Southampton and
Bristol City. Netted 11 goals in 52 games for Scotland.

GREAVSIE ASSESSMENT: 'Joe was a crash-bang centre-forward who looked a fearsome sight with his front four teeth missing. But, along with his physical strength and heading power, Joe had a good footballing brain and was brilliant at bringing his supporting strikers into the game with clever lay-offs and subtle touches. I would loved to have played alongside him at my peak because I know I could have fed off all his hard work. For all the goals he scored, he made many more for others.

He created a unique record when he became the only Scot to score in three World Cups – 1974, 1978 and 1982. Always a keen student of football tactics, Joe – or Jaws as he was known to clubmates – tried his hand at managing with Bristol City, Hearts and – in a caretaker capacity – Portsmouth. But it is as a No 2 that he shines, and he is an influential right-hand man to Harry Redknapp at Tottenham.´

JOE JORDAN'S Most Memorable Goal

MATCH: Scotland v. Czechoslovakia at Hampden Park
SEASON: 1974 World Cup qualifying match

'I was sent on as substitute with the score deadlocked at 1-1, and I managed to score with almost my first touch. Willie Morgan crossed the ball from the right and I dived forward in a crowded penalty area to head the ball into the net. The goal clinched Scotland's place in the World Cup finals in Germany, where we were unlucky to be eliminated without losing a game. I scored our second goal in a 2-0 win over Zaire and a last-minute equaliser against Yugoslavia. We held defending champions Brazil to a goalless draw, but finished third in our group behind the Brazilians and Yugoslavia. We were devastated. So near, yet so far.'

33. TREVOR FRANCIS

FACTFILE: Born Plymouth, April 19 1954
Career span: 1971-94. Made his debut for Birmingham City aged 16 and scored 15 goals in his first 15 games. Brian Clough made him Britain's first £1 million footballer when he bought him for Nottingham Forest in 1979. Climaxed his first season with Forest by scoring the goal that won the 1979 European Cup final. Also played for Detroit Express, Manchester City, Sampdoria, Atalanta, Rangers, Wollongong City, QPR and Sheffield Wednesday. Scored 12 goals in 52 England games, and 233 in 629 world-wide matches.

GREAVSIE ASSESSMENT: `Trevor had the sharp reactions, close control and acceleration powers of a born goalscorer, and proved he also had strong character by refusing to let a severe Achilles injury curb his appetite for the game. Fabio Capello says that he is the finest English footballer ever to play in Serie A, which is quite a testimony considering he was past his peak by the time he joined Sampdoria. He was equally efficient and effective as a midfield player, but I preferred to see him going forward into the box and taking on defenders. When on those sort of raiding runs he was exceptional.

The football bug bit him hard and he could not let go, and he had some bruising experiences as a manager with Sheffield Wednesday, Birmingham City and Crystal Palace before being sensible and settling for talking about the game with authority as resident pundit for Al Jazeera TV Sports. It's much easier in the armchair!´

TREVOR FRANCIS' Most Memorable Goal
MATCH: Blackpool v. Birmingham City
SEASON: 1971-72, Second Division

•It was my second season in the first-team and I was still learning the game. Bob Latchford won the ball and headed it down to me. I was about 30 yards from goal and hit a reflex shot on the half-volley. It was as sweet a connection as I ever made. It left me like a rocket and landed on target in the top right-hand corner of the net. One of the most important goals I ever scored was, of course, the headed winner for Nottingham Forest in the 1979 European Cup final. Suddenly the weight of being the first million-pound player did not feel quite as heavy because I had given Brian Clough the major trophy that made my transfer worthwhile.•

Trevor Francis, British football's first million-pound player

Andy Gray, for whom the Sky was the limit in his playing days

> **FACTFILE:** Born Glasgow, November 30 1955
> Career span: 1973-90. Became British football's most
> expensive player when Wolves paid £1,175,000 to Aston
> Villa for him in 1969. Scored 36 Scottish League goals for
> his first club Dundee United and 54 goals for Villa in 113
> League games. A League Cup final winner with Villa (1977)
> and Wolves (1980). In two seasons with Everton (1983-
> 85) he collected winners' medals in the FA Cup, League
> championship and Cup Winners' Cup. Returned to Villa and
> later played for Notts County, WBA and Rangers.

GREAVSIE ASSESSMENT: `These days Andy talks a good game on Sky, but he could also play the game better than most. He was not the most skilful centre-forward, but his aggression, determination and courage made him a constant dangerman to even the tightest defences. He was a real 90-minute battler and when paired with John Richards at Wolves and then fellow-Scot Graeme Sharp at Everton, he could produce moments that old masters like Lofthouse, Lawton and Dean would have been proud to match.

The way he gives an interesting and authoritative analysis of matches for Sky suggests that he was some sort of tactical genius as a player but, out on the pitch, he played it rough and tough like a man quarried from the pavements of Glasgow. We all sat up and took notice of him when he won both the PFA Young Player and Player of the Year awards in 1977. You didn't need a TV replay to know that young Andy was a bit special.´

ANDY GRAY'S Most Memorable Goal

MATCH: Wolves v. Borussia Moenchengladbach
SEASON: 1980, pre-season club tournament

•I was standing at the extreme left-hand corner of the 18-yard box. A shot was blocked and the ball came bouncing towards me. I met it first time on the half-volley with the outside of my left foot. As it left me, the ball was on course with the photographers to the left of the far post. But I had put so much swerve on it that as it began to rise it went on a curve and finished up in the postage-stamp corner of the net. I scored many more important goals in more vital matches, but this was by far the best goal I ever scored and I just wish I had it on tape to play to people to show just how skilful I was – even if it was something of a freak moment in my career!•

FACTFILE: Born Nottingham, December 6 1956
Career span: 1973-90. Went on loan from Nottingham Forest to Lincoln and Doncaster before emerging as a key man in the Forest team that won the League title in 1978 and the European Cup the next season. Moved to FC Cologne for £500,000 in 1979, scoring 28 goals in 81 Bundesliga games. Won 42 England caps (16 goals). Returned to England with Arsenal where in 131 League matches he scored 56 goals. Back in Germany, he played in Cologne and became a coach and then a successful businessman.

GREAVSIE ASSESSMENT: `Tony's early experiences of being shunted around did nothing for his confidence, but once he began to get belief in himself when Brian Clough arrived at Forest, he developed into one of the best-equipped strikers in the game. His combination at club and country level with Trevor Francis was rich with skill and invention.

He became a more sophisticated and subtle player following his taste of football in West Germany and, by the time he joined Arsenal, he was was the finished article. For the next four seasons he was the top marksman for the Gunners, including five in a single game against Aston Villa, until injury robbed him of a vital half yard of pace.

Tony always had a sharp brain, and turned it to the pursuit of profit in a succession of business interests, including a sports media project in partnership with former Forest and England team-mate Viv Anderson.´

TONY WOODCOCK'S Most Memorable Goal

MATCH: Nottingham Forest v. Southampton at Wembley
SEASON: 1979 League Cup final

•It's not so much a goal as a game that stands out in my memory. Forest were trailing 1-0 to Southampton at half-time and as we came off I thought to myself, 'We're going to get a rocket from the boss.' But all Brian Clough said to us was, "Have a nice cup of tea and relax lads. All I want from you in the second-half is that you pass only to players wearing a red shirt, then everything will be fine." That's all he said. He was an absolute master of motivation, and we went out and won 3-2, and I clinched the victory late in the game, dinking the ball into the net after exchanging passes with Archie Gemmill. It was the day I realised Cloughie was a genius.•

Tony Woodcock, a goalscoring star in the Football League and the Bundesliga

Gary Lineker, deadly in the penalty area

FACTFILE: Born Leicester, November 30 1960
Career span: 1978-1994. A prolific goalscorer with Leicester
(96), Everton (30), Barcelona (42) and Tottenham (67),
before finishing in Japan with Grampus Eight (9 goals)
when a toe injury ended his career. Won the Copa del Rey
in 1988 and the European Cup Winners' Cup in 1989 with
Barcelona and the FA Cup with Spurs in 1991. Scored 48
goals in 80 England games. He was top scorer at the 1986
World Cup and is also the only player to have won the
English Golden Boot with three different clubs.

GREAVSIE ASSESSMENT: `I won't say anything corny about Gary being a crisp finisher, but he certainly knew the way to goal and scored goals wherever he took his boots. He was not the most flamboyant of players but deadly in the penalty area, where his positioning, pace, anticipation and finishing accuracy made him a handful for any defence. In his peak years he was one of the great untouchables, as he proved with his goals at the 1986 World Cup, a hat-trick against Real Madrid for Barcelona and a typically spirited display leading the England attack at Italia 90.

Gary has since become an excellent anchorman of the BBC's flagship Match of the Day show, and has made a fortune with his commercials for Walkers Crisps. He was never booked throughout his career and was always a sporting opponent and a fine ambassador for the game that he always played with determination and dedication.´

GARY LINEKER'S Most Memorable Goal

MATCH: England v. West Germany in Turin
SEASON: 1990 World Cup semi-final

❛It was the 80th minute and we were trailing 1-0, when Paul Parker made a thrusting run down the right. I had two German defenders accompanying me but I managed to confuse them by making a sudden darting run to get in first to meet Paul's hip-high cross. I controlled the ball with my thigh, pushed it out to my left and then hit it in full stride with my left foot to send it under a sliding defender and into the far corner of the net. We were euphoric and could almost taste the World Cup final, but then we had the devastating disappointment of losing the penalty shoot-out. So while I was thrilled with my goal it proved to be no real consolation for our defeat.❜

FACTFILE: Born Newcastle, January 18 1961
Career span: 1979-1999. Scored 237 League goals in 755
appearances after being released as a teenager by Newcastle.
He went on to play for Carlisle (22 goals), Vancouver
White Caps (28), Newcastle (108), Liverpool (46), Everton
(25), Bolton (2), Fulham (4), Hartlepool (2) and finishing
with two games for Melbourne Knights. He was also briefly
with Man United and Man City. Scored nine goals in 59
England games. Collected two First Division titles and an
FA Cup winners' medal with Liverpool in 1989.

GREAVSIE ASSESSMENT: `Peter was quick, skilful and incisive, at his best when playing a supporting role to a main striker. Gary Lineker described him as the best partner he ever had during their days gathering goals for England. Kevin Keegan, who played alongside him and brought him back to St James' Park when he became manager, said Peter made team-mates seem better than they were by creating space for them with his clever movement off the ball.

He was a maker as well as a taker of goals, and created many goals for team-mates while helping himself to more than 250 goals in all competitions. He was idolised on Tyneside, and was one of the few players who appeared for both Liverpool and Everton. His nine goals in 59 games for England does not tell the story of his input. Time and again when a goal was analysed, Peter was found to have played an assist part. He was a players' player and, during his career, sold more dummies than Mothercare.´

PETER BEARDSLEY'S Most Memorable Goal
MATCH: Portsmouth v. Newcastle United
SEASON: 1983-84, Second Division

'The one that sticks in my memory was at Fratton Park when we were chasing promotion. Kevin Keegan – thanks very much – gave me a hospital pass on a mudheap of a pitch. Thinking of preservation, I dummied my way round the centre-half who was coming at me like a train, and then sent the goalkeeper the wrong way. Out of the corner of my eye I saw the full-back coming at full speed with me as his target. I just stood still and waited, knowing there was every chance he'd boot the ball into his own net. As I stood with my foot on the ball he slid past me without making contact, and I then calmly steered the ball into the net for one of my favourite goals of all time.'

Peter Beardsley, who sold more dummies than Mothercare

Ian Rush, first British player to win the European Golden Boot

FACTFILE: Born St Asaph, Wales, October 20 1961
Career span: 1979-2000. His clubs Chester City (14 goals),
Liverpool 1980-87 and 1988-96 (469 League games, 229
goals), Juventus (7 goals), Leeds United (3 goals), Newcastle United (0), Sheffield United, loan (4),Wrexham (0),
Sydney Olympic (1 goal). Club honours: 5 League championships, 3 FA Cups, 5 League Cups, 1 European Cup. Wales:
73 caps, 28 goals. 1984: European Golden Boot, Footballer
of the Year, PFA Player of the Year. In total, he scored
346 goals in 660 Liverpool appearances.

GREAVSIE ASSESSMENT: ´Ian knew only one way to play the game: Go for goal! He was devastating in the last third of the pitch, particularly when he had Kenny Dalglish alongside him as a plundering partner. He had a golden season in 1983-84, winning just about everything in sight. He pulled off the individual hat-trick of winning the FWA and PFA footballer of the year awards, plus he became the first Brit to win the Golden Boot as Europe's top scorer. All this in a season when unstoppable Liverpool captured the treble of League championship, League Cup and European Cup. His input was 49 goals!

He once went an incredible 145 matches for Liverpool without being on the losing side. Ian joined Juventus for £3 million in 1986, but suffered home sickness and was soon back at Anfield, where he had to battle for his old place against a formidable challenge from John Aldridge. I would rate only John Charles and Ryan Giggs ahead of him as the greatest of all Welsh players.´

IAN RUSH'S Most Memorable Goal
MATCH: Liverpool 3, Everton 1 at Wembley
SEASON: 1986 FA Cup final

•The one that has stuck in my memory above all others was my first equaliser in the 1986 FA Cup final against our neighbours Everton. Every time I had scored for Liverpool, we had been unbeaten. In the papers the next day, Gary Lineker said, 'As soon as Ian Rush scored, we knew we weren't going to win.' So I realised that after I scored, the Liverpool players were lifted and the Everton players put their heads down. I think that was more of a mental thing. One paper said, 'It was the first equaliser to win the FA Cup final.' We seemed to get bigger and stronger after that and Everton were deflated, so you can see why I like to remember that one!•

Ally McCoist, a flop at Sunderland ... a legend at Rangers

FACTFILE: Born Bellshill, September 24 1962
Career span: 1979-2001. Began his career with St Johnstone
(22 goals) before moving to Sunderland in 1981. He returned
to Scotland two years later and signed with Rangers after
scoring just eight goals in 56 League games. Netted a total
355 goals for Rangers, including a record 251 Scottish
League goals in 418 games. Added another 12 goals to his
collection in a two-season wind-down at Kilmarnock. Won
61 Scottish international caps, scoring 19 goals. Won ten
Scottish championships and nine League Cups.

GREAVSIE ASSESSMENT: `The teenage Ally who flopped at Sunderland grew up to become one of Scotland's greatest ever goalscorers. His incredible record at Ibrox is all the evidence you need that he was a natural predator. During his 15 years with Rangers he became the first player to be Europe's top goalscorer twice in a row. Oddly, his eight goals while at Sunderland included a hat-trick of penalties in a League game against West Bromwich Albion.

Ally became best known in England as a bubbly team captain on *A Question of Sport* and as a regular pundit on ITV. But all the time he was building a new career in broadcasting he was pining for football, and he returned to Scotland as assistant manager at Rangers, where he is a living legend. As we were preparing this book it was announced that Ally will get his dream job in 2011 – manager of the Rangers club for whom he has scored more goals than any other player.´

ALLY McCOIST'S Most Memorable Goal
MATCH: Rangers v. Celtic at Hampden Park
SEASON: 1992 Scottish Cup semi-final

•It was a wild, wet and windy night at Hampden and we were deep in trouble. We were down to ten men from the sixth minute after David Robertson had been sent off for a bodycheck. We had never scored against Celtic in a Scottish Cup tie for twenty years, and all the odds were against us. We made a break in the last minute of the first-half, and Stuart McCall made a magnificent run down the right before squaring the ball to me as I raced to the edge of the Celtic penalty area. I shot instantly and the ball went low into the net off the left post. We hung on to win 1-0, and went on to beat Airdrie in the final, my only Scottish Cup winners' medal.•

```
FACTFILE: Born Wrexham, Wales, November 1 1963
Career span: 1980-2002. Had two spells with Manchester
United (119 goals in 345 League games. Also played for
Barcelona (4 La Liga goals), Bayern Munich (6 Bundesliga
goals), Chelsea (25 goals), Southampton (2 goals), Ever-
ton (1 goal) and Blackburn Rovers (6 goals), before re-
tiring in 2002. Scored 16 goals in 72 games for Wales.
His medals haul included two Premier League title medals,
four FA Cups, three League Cups and two European Cup Win-
ners' Cups.
```

GREAVSIE ASSESSMENT: 'The nickname Sparky was given to Mark when he was a Wrexham schoolboy, but it fitted him perfectly as a player. He could electrify a game with a sudden surge, and also had a sparky temper if being kicked about in an era when the game was still about physical contact. Mark was a combative centre-forward famed and feared as much for his fierce aggression as for a potent right foot. He led his line with intelligence, was skilled at laying off the ball and then going for the return pass, and had powers of acceleration that took him past defenders as he went through the gears.

With every manager he played for, Mark quietly picked up tips and tucked them away ready for his switch to management. He has managed Wales, Blackburn, Manchester City and Fulham, and is building the sort of experience that could make him a contender for the Old Trafford hot seat when Sir Alex finally bows out.'

MARK HUGHES' Most Memorable Goal

MATCH: Manchester United 2, Barcelona 1 in Rotterdam
SEASON: 1991 European Cup Winners' Cup final

'I suppose the best goals are the ones people remember, and people always remind me of two in particular – the goal against Oldham in the FA Cup semi-final and the Cup Winners' Cup goal against Barcelona. They were not technically my favourite goals, but because so many people remember them – plus the Wales goal against Spain – they are the ones that stay fresh in the memory. I guess I'd have to say the goal against Barcelona was the most satisfying, because I didn't have a particularly successful time with them. I scored both our goals, and the second one was a bit special. It was from an acute angle and I had to spin the ball off the outside of my boot.'

Mark Hughes, who had two productive spells with Manchester United

Ian Wright, thumbs up for a top Gunner

> **FACTFILE:** Born Woolwich, November 3 1963
> Career span: 1985-2000. Was a plasterer while playing non-league football at Dulwich Hamlet when signed by Crystal Palace at the age of 21. Scored 90 goals for Palace in 225 League games, then had his greatest days at Arsenal (128 goals in 221 League matches). With the Gunners, he lifted the Premier League title and both major domestic Cup trophies, plus the European Cup Winners' Cup. Scored nine goals in 33 England games, and played briefly for West Ham, Nottingham Forest, Celtic and Burnley.

GREAVSIE ASSESSMENT: `Ian had a bit of a fairytale career, and looked to have missed his chance when Millwall, Southend and Brighton gave him a thumbs down. The turning point for him was when that excellent manager Steve Coppell spotted his potential at Crystal Palace, paired him with Mark Bright and from then on he played as if trying to make up for lost time and determined not to go back to a life as a plasterer.

He had blistering pace, vicious shooting power, loads of energy and enthusiasm and his passion and hunger showed in every game he played. He did a fantastic job for George Graham in turning his turgid Arsenal team into a side with an edge, and it was his drive and determination that turned the Gunners into trophy winners.

Ian carried his enthusiasm into the world of television and he has made an impact with his outspoken comments on TV and radio.´

IAN WRIGHT'S Most Memorable Goal

MATCH: Arsenal v. Everton

SEASON: 1993-94 Premier League

•I was already on the scoresheet against Everton when David Seaman hammered a long clearance downfield. It just cleared the head of Gary Ablett and I saw my chance and raced on to the bouncing ball. I flicked it up, flicked it up again and then again as the Everton defenders tackled and missed me. The wide figure of goalkeeper Neville Southall was coming towards me and I flicked the ball yet again, this time over his head and into the net. I don't think I'll ever forget the look on big Nev's face. He just could not believe what had happened to him. I ran to the new North Bank Stand and hugged the fans in the front row. Everybody went potty. Unforgettable!•

42. TEDDY SHERINGHAM

FACTFILE: Born Highams Park, London, April 2 1966 Career span: 1983-2008. Laid the foundation to his career at Millwall (93 goals, 220 League games). Later played for Nottingham Forest (14 League goals), Tottenham (two spells, 98), Man United (31), Portsmouth (9), West Ham (28) and finishing at Colchester at the age of 42 in 2007-08 (3). Won the League, FA Cup and Champions League treble with Manchester United in 1998-99 and scored 11 goals in 51 England appearances. Netted a total 289 goals in 760 domestic League games.

GREAVSIE ASSESSMENT: `Teddy was one of those sophisticated players whose astute passing and running brought the players around him into the game. He gained notoriety beyond the football pitch by being the player featured in the infamous 'Bung' court case in which Alan Sugar pointed a finger at the fiddling that goes on in football. But Teddy didn't fiddle around on the pitch, and as well as being a prolific goalscorer made many more with his clever positioning and intelligent use of the ball.

He and Jurgen Klinsmann had a potent partnership at Spurs, but it was at Old Trafford where he left his biggest mark. Typical, you wait 15 years for a title to come along and then three trophies arrive at once. In a mad climax to the 1998-99 season, he helped Man United win the League championship, FA Cup and dramatically scored one goal and made the winner in the dying moments of the Champions League final. Teddy boy had become a legend.´

TEDDY SHERINGHAM'S Most Memorable Goal
MATCH: Manchester United v. Bayern Munich at the Nou Camp
SEASON: 1999 Champions League final

⁶I came off the substitute's bench to score a stoppage-time equaliser against Bayern Munich in the Nou Camp. It was a snatched, scrappy goal, but the most important I ever scored. A few moments later I flicked the ball on in a crowded penalty area for Ole Gunnar Solskjær to score a last-minute winner and complete the treble of the Premier League, FA Cup and European Cup. From not having won a major trophy, I suddenly had all three top honours, and the icing on the cake was that the football writers' and the PFA elected me their footballer of the year. You could not have made it up.⁹

The European Cup goes to Teddy Sheringham's head

'Sir Les' Ferdinand, a have-boots-will-travel hit man

Greavsie's Greatest: *43. LES FERDINAND*

FACTFILE: Born Paddington, December 8 1966
Career span: 1986-2006. Missed the usual schoolboys
scouting net and was picked up by QPR when playing non-
League football for Hayes. Became the first player to score
Premier League goals for six different clubs while playing
for QPR (80 League goals), Newcastle (41), Tottenham (33),
West Ham (2), Leicester City (12) and Bolton (1). Also
played on loan with Brentford and Turkish club Besiktas,
and wound down his career with Reading and then Watford.
Scored five goals in 17 England appearances.

GREAVSIE ASSESSMENT: `'Sir Les' – as he is known to many fans – was a have-boots-will-travel professional hit man, who could always be counted on to come up with the goods, in his case the goals. He was graceful and elegant for such a powerfully built man, and he even managed to look cool when making aerial challenges – the best at hanging in the air since Denis Law.

I thought Les was at his most impressive when in harness with Alan Shearer at Newcastle, and the Premier League has rarely seen a more productive and potent partnership. It took a long time but he got the recognition he deserved when his fellow professionals named him PFA Player of the Year in 1996.

In my peak playing years, Les was just the sort of partner I would have enjoyed playing alongside, letting him do the physical stuff while I picked up the pieces. While at school he used to play in goal before converting to centre-forward. What a loss that would have been to the goalscorers' union.´

LES FERDINAND'S Most Memorable Goal

MATCH: Manchester United v. Tottenham
SEASON: 1998-99 Premier League

•I'll always remember the goal that I scored at Old Trafford against Peter Schmeichel with mixed feelings. It was the year Arsenal and United went into the final game of the season dead level – and if we'd have beaten United, Arsenal would have won the title. I lobbed the ball over Peter Schmeichel in the first-half and turned Old Trafford as quiet as a cemetery. It was a cracker, even if I say it myself. News of the goal reached Highbury and the Arsenal supporters were singing my name. It must have been the first time a Spurs player's name was sung by Gooners. Cole and Beckham scored to give United victory and the title, and saved me being lynched by Spurs supporters!•

44. MATTHEW LE TISSIER

FACTFILE: Born St Peter Port, Guernsey, December 8 1966 Career span: 1986-2002. A one-club loyalist, who played for Southampton throughout his career. Scored 162 goals in 443 League games, second-highest ever scorer for Southampton behind Mick Channon. Voted PFA Young Player of the Year in 1990. He was the first non-out-and-out striker to score 100 goals in the Premier League. Famous for his accuracy from the penalty spot, converting from the spot 48 times from 49 attempts. Won 21 England Under-21 caps (3 goals) and six at senior level, but without finding the net.

GREAVSIE ASSESSMENT: `One of the few forwards who was not an out-and-out striker to make it into my top fifty, mainly because goals were his business – and usually of the spectacular variety. He was one of the cleanest strikers of a ball in modern football, and it was disappointing that in his few full England appearances he failed to get on the scoresheet.

While I admired Matt for his loyalty, it definitely cost him a much more productive international career. Had he given in to one of the many approaches that came his way from major clubs – and in particular Tottenham in the early 1990s – I am convinced he would have became a permanent fixture in the England team. And he would have been No 1 choice in penalty shoot-outs!

He gave the impression of being casual and laid-back, but there are a procession of goalkeepers who have waved to the ball on its way into the net who will confirm that he had thunderous power in his right foot.´

MATTHEW LE TISSIER'S Most Memorable Goal
MATCH: Blackburn Rovers v. Southampton
SEASON: 1994-95, Premier League

❛The goal I always bang on about is the one against Blackburn Rovers at Ewood Park that I scored from about 35 yards against my old mate Timmy Flowers. I teed the ball up and volleyed it past him while everybody was expecting me to either pass or bring the ball forward. Tim gets sick and tired every time I mention it, and every time it pops up on television or on a goals-collection DVD. When he catches me mentioning it, he sends me an instant text message saying, 'Will you stop going on about that f****** goal, you lost the game 3-2, get over it!' He has got a point. And they did go on to win the Premier League title that season ... but it *was* a belting goal!❜

Matthew Le Tissier, who specialised in goals of the spectacular variety

Alan Shearer, the No 9 who was No 1 for Newcastle and England

FACTFILE: Born Gosforth, Newcastle, August 13 1970 Career span: 1986-2006. Clubs: Southampton 1986-88 (118 League games, 23 goals), Blackburn Rovers 1992-96 (138 League games, 112 goals), Newcastle United 1996-2006 (303 League games, 148 goals). Won Premier League title with Blackburn (1994-95). England: 63 caps, 30 goals (34 games as captain). Euro 96 Golden Boot winner. Highest ever Premier League scorer with 260 goals. Footballer of the Year 1994, PFA Player of the Year 1995 and 1997. Briefly Newcastle manager in 2009. BBC Match of the Day pundit.

GREAVSIE ASSESSMENT: `There are a mountain of goals as evidence that Alan Shearer deserves a prominent place in my top fifty. Cut him and I am sure he would bleed Newcastle black and white, but Alan was a long time coming home. The Geordies turned him down at the age of fifteen, famously putting him in goal for part of his trial. Southampton recognised a goalscorer when they saw one, and he repaid their faith by scoring a hat-trick at the age of seventeen in his first full First Division match against Arsenal. It was just the start of the flood of goals.

There were many technically more gifted players than Shearer, but few could equal his physical presence in the penalty area that had something of the old school about it. Come to think of it, he could be one of the last physical contact players we see at top level as referees come down more and more on any player showing a sniff of aggression.´

ALAN SHEARER'S Most Memorable Goal
MATCH: Newcastle United v. Portsmouth
SEASON: 2005-06 Premier League

ʻThe goal that gave me most satisfaction was the 201st Newcastle goal that took me past the Jackie Milburn record. I had scored more spectacular goals but this had such special meaning. I had grown up with the Milburn legend ringing in my ears. My Dad was a great fan of his, and I realised just how much my goal meant when the Newcastle fans were still chanting my name five minutes after I'd put the ball into the net. It sent a shiver down my spine. I consider it a privilege and an honour just to be mentioned in the same breath as Wor Jackie. To have overtaken him in the record books means so much to me. You have to be a Geordie to know what I'm talking about.ʼ

Greavsie's Greatest: 46. ANDY COLE

FACTFILE: Born Nottingham, October 15 1971
Career span: 1989-2008. Second-highest goalscorer in
Premier League history to Alan Shearer after being let
go by Arsenal after only one match. Scored 187 Premier
goals. Honours include PFA Young Player of the Year, five
Premier titles, two FA Cup and one Champions League.
Capped 15 times by England, one goal. Clubs: Arsenal,
Fulham (15 goals), Bristol City (20), Newcastle (55), Man
United (93), Blackburn (27), Man City (22), Portsmouth
(3), Birmingham (1), Burnley (6), Nottingham Forest.

GREAVSIE ASSESSMENT: `What a gaffe Arsenal made when they let Andy go after only one match. He developed into one of the sharpest and most devastating finishers in the modern game. Well balanced and explosive over short distances, he could dismantle any defence with his pace and power and was a supreme poacher. A real fox in the box. He had an electric partnership with Peter Beardsley, and it made no sense to me when Kevin Keegan sold him to Man United after he had scored 68 goals in 84 League games.

Andy had the character to make a comeback after Razor Ruddock had managed to break both his legs and, while he lost some of his speed, he was still a dangerman in the penalty box. One of the mysteries is why he did not do better at international level. I would not have thought it possible that he could play 15 times for England and score only one goal. King Cole was an obvious nickname for him. He lived up to it, except in an England shirt.´

ANDY COLE'S Most Memorable Goal
MATCH: Barcelona v. Manchester United
SEASON: 1998-99 Champions League, group match

•I had the striker's attitude that any time you got the ball over the goal-line it was memorable. There were several bicycle kick goals that pleased me, but the one that gave me greatest satisfaction was at the Nou Camp in the Champions League. Dwight Yorke and I had an almost telepathic understanding, and we cut through the Barcelona defence like a knife through butter with a series of one-twos before I thumped the ball into the net from just inside the penalty box. It was sheer perfection. We were back in the Nou Camp for the Champions League final when we completed the treble in the most fantastic finish I have ever known to a match.❜

Andy Cole, released by Arsenal after just one game

Art Turner
2010

Robbie Fowler, a born goalscorer who was often the companion of controversy

FACTFILE: Born Toxteth, April 9 1975
Career span: 1993 - present. Best known for two spells
with his local club Liverpool (128 goals), he has also
travelled the football roundabout with Leeds (14 League
goals), Manchester City (20), Cardiff City (4), and then
Blackburn before continuing his career in Australia with
North Queensland Fury and Perth Glory. Played 26 times
for England and scored seven goals. He was voted PFA Young
Player of the Year two years in a row, and in 2001 won the
FA Cup, League Cup and Uefa Cup treble with Liverpool.

GREAVSIE ASSESSMENT: `Robbie was a born goalscorer, one of the finest natural finishers of the last twenty years. Unfortunately, his ability was too often overshadowed by controversy. There was the unsavoury incident when he mimed snorting the byline as if it were a line of cocaine, a training ground bust-up with Liverpool coach and old Anfield hero Phil Thompson, a fine for flashing his bum at Chelsea defender Graeme Le Saux, and rumoured playboy antics with a clique of Liverpool players nicknamed the Spice Boys.

But, when he was in the headlines for football, it was because of his razor-sharp work in the penalty area, where he had few equals for turning a half chance into a goal in the blinking of an eye. His partnerships with Steve McManaman and Stan Collymore were special but not long enough to reach full potential. I'm sure when he looks back on his career he will feel he should have achieved more considering the ability with which he was blessed.´

ROBBIE FOWLER'S Most Memorable Goal
MATCH: Liverpool v. Aston Villa
SEASON: 1994-95 Premier League

`I collected a clearance out of defence with my back to the Villa goal, about 35 yards out. Villa defender Steve Staunton moved in on me and I back-heeled the ball through his legs. Then with the Villa defenders and my own team-mates expecting me to pass I let fly with a left foot shot. The ball left me like a rocket and beat Villa goalkeeper Mark Bosnich all ends up. Mark told the press afterwards that he couldn't believe it because I had hardly used any back lift. It was one of two goals I scored that day and we beat Villa 3-2. I was lucky to score lots of goals, but that is one that gave me tremendous satisfaction because I was so far out.´

FACTFILE: Born Chester, Cheshire, December 14 1979
Career span: 1996 - present.
Clubs: Liverpool 1996-2004 (216 League games, 118 goals),
Real Madrid 2004-05 (36 League games, 13 goals), Newcastle
United 2005-09 (71 League games, 26 goals), Manchester
United (4 goals at the time of publication). Club honours:
1 FA Cup winners' medal, 2 League Cups, 1 Uefa Cup.
England: 89 caps, 40 goals. BBC Sports Personality of the
Year 1998. PFA Young Player of the Year 1998. European
Footballer of the Year 2001.

GREAVSIE ASSESSMENT: `Since retiring, I've continually seen young footballers described as the 'new' Jimmy Greaves. The only time I've considered that close to a fair description was when Michael Owen first emerged at Liverpool. I could see a mirror image of myself at the same age. We both made our first-team debuts at 17, Michael for Liverpool and me for Chelsea. We were of a similar build, stocky and with the same low centre of gravity. I was strongly reminded of myself by his ball control and his ability to wrong foot defenders with his acceleration and sudden changes of direction. When it kept being put to me that he was the 'new' me, I always made a point of saying, 'No, he is the one and only Michael Owen, his own man.' I have watched his career with close interest, and only a succession of awful injuries have prevented him becoming arguably England's finest ever striker. I got off the merry-go-round at 31. I wonder how much longer Michael will punish his body?´

MICHAEL OWEN'S Most Memorable Goal
MATCH: England v. Scotland at Newcastle
SEASON: 1994 Victory Shield Under-15s international

`Obviously my goal against Argentina at the 1998 World Cup has a special place in my memory but, before that, my favourite goal was one I scored for England's Under-15s at St James' Park. We were playing Scotland and they'd just made it 1-1. I was standing on the centre spot for the kick-off, the ball was tapped to me and straight away I set off on the sort of run that I repeated against Argentina four years later. I beat about four Scottish players and pass-shot the ball wide of the keeper. Sky were televising it, so I got to see it afterwards. We ended up winning the game 2-1 and won the Victory Shield as well. All these years later, I get a warm feeling when I think of it.`

Michael Owen, cursed by a succession of awful injuries

Jermain Defoe, one of the most dangerous and decisive finishers in the modern game

FACTFILE: Born Becton, East London, October 7 1982 Career span: 1999-present. Began his career with the Charlton Athletic youth team before moving to West Ham United aged sixteen. Selected for his West Ham debut by manager Harry Redknapp in 2000, and after a season-long loan spell at Bournemouth established himself with the Hammers. Moved to Spurs in 2004. Joined Portsmouth in 2008 and returned to White Hart Lane in 2009 and was reunited with Redknapp. Made his England debut in 2004 and as of October 2010, has made 45 appearances, scoring 15 goals.

GREAVSIE ASSESSMENT: `Inconsistent, but when on his game Jermain is one of the most dangerous and decisive finishers in the modern game. He plays off the front man with dash and daring, and is particularly potent when paired with the human stepladder that is Peter Crouch and with jet-paced Aaron Lennon feeding him with crosses from the right-wing. He has been unlucky with a spate of injuries, but when fully fit can send defences into panic mode with his pace and positioning.

My old mate Harry Redknapp has been going on about Defoe for ages and he gets no argument from me when he calls him the best finisher England have had for several years. Jermain is no longer a kid and I would now like to see him taking more responsibility and bossing the penalty area, rather than waiting to pick up the pieces. He is a top-notch striker, but I believe he can be even better. For England's sake, let's hope so.´

JERMAIN DEFOE'S Most Memorable Goal

MATCH: Tottenham v. Wigan
SEASON: 2009-10 Premier League

•It's five goals rather than one that will always stay in my memory! We were leading Wigan 1-0 at half-time and the final score was 9-1, and I'd been lucky enough to have scored five of the second-half goals – including a hat-trick inside seven minutes. Once the fifth goal went in, I started thinking about the double hat-trick. As I went to the touchline, our coach Joe Jordan shouted, 'Go for it ... go for the sixth.' I looked up and saw there were a few minutes left, so I knew it was on. That's how it is when you're on fire as a goalscorer. You always want the NEXT one. It was a like a wonderful dream and you don't want to wake up, brilliant.•

Greavsie's Greatest: 50. WAYNE ROONEY

FACTFILE: Born Croxteth, Liverpool, October 24 1985
Career span: 2000- present.
Clubs: Everton 2000-04 (67 Premier League games, 15 goals),
Manchester United 2004 - present (as at publication: 193
Premier League games, 92 goals). Made Everton debut at 16
and scored against Arsenal. Club honours: Premier League
three times, the 2007-08 UEFA Champions League and two
League Cups. He has also been awarded the PFA Players
Player of the Year and the FWA Footballer of the Year in
2009-10. England caps to date: 67, 26 goals.

GREAVSIE ASSESSMENT: `The 'Baby' of my list, who has the potential to become one of the best there has ever been. There's no doubt whatsoever about his talent. That has been given to him by the footballing gods. The question is, does he have the temperament to fulfil all his rich promise? Rooney plays his football on the edge, and you always sense that he is an earthquake waiting to happen. Rival defenders know that he has a tinderbox temper, and it is easy to imagine managers giving pre-match instructions: 'Wind Rooney up.'

Wayne is the most naturally gifted footballer to emerge on the English scene for years. An instinctive genius, he produces magical moments without really knowing himself how he has done it. He is dogged by controversies in his private life and seemed just a shadow of himself in the 2010 World Cup. I just hope the best is still to come but as we were going to press there was a question mark over his future with Man United. The boy is a walking headline.´

WAYNE ROONEY'S Most Memorable Goal
MATCH: Manchester United v. Newcastle
SEASON: 2004-05 Premier League

•I'd just been in trouble with the referee who booked me and I was involved in an argument with Alan Shearer. I was really wound-up when the ball dropped in front of me. I didn't stop to think, just hit it as hard as I could. I was about 25 yards out and the ball flew into the top corner past Shay Given in the Newcastle goal. It was at the Stretford End and there was an enormous roar as the ball hit the net. The one that counted most for the team was against Manchester City in the Carling Cup semi-final. It was a massive game for us, and I managed to score with a header in the last minute to send us into the final, just as City thought they were taking us into extra-time.•

Wayne Rooney, dogged by controversies in his private life

FACTFILE: Inverness, January 8 1947
Career span: 1966-80. Liverpool let him go on a free
transfer to York City, and he then launched a spectacular
scoring spree. He gathered 256 League goals with York
(34), Bournemouth (103), Manchester United (5), West Ham
(5), Norwich (51), Southampton (42) and Bournemouth again
(16), before 13 games as Blackpool player-coach. His nine
goals for Bournemouth in an FA Cup tie against Margate in
1971 remains an FA Cup individual scoring record. Capped
seven times by Scotland. Now coaches in the USA.

GREAVSIE ASSESSMENT: `What's this, number fifty-one? I have added Ted to my original list to stop my manager/agent/publisher Terry Baker grumbling because I have left out one of his heroes. I tossed up between Ted and Peter Beardsley as to which of them should get the 50th place in my final line-up, and on reflection, I feel I should include Ted. So my Top 50 has become my Top 51. It's MY book so I will make up my own rules! Ted, of course, came to prominence with those nine goals for Bournemouth in an FA Cup tie against Margate, and he was a prolific goalscorer throughout his career after Liverpool had dropped a clanger by letting him go without giving him a proper chance to show his pace and power. Ted was at his most potent when in partnership with Phil Boyer. They were a dynamic duo together for York City, Bournemouth, Norwich and Southampton, with Ted the brawn and Boyer the brains in an impressive double act. He was a born goalscorer.´

TED MacDOUGALL'S Most Memorable Goal
MATCH: Aston Villa v. Bournemouth
SEASON: 1970-71, Third Division

'The ball was played infield to me from our left-back just inside the Villa half. I laid it off first time to our right-winger Tony Scott, and I then made my way at speed to the far post. Tony played an early ball to the near post, and I suddenly changed direction and dived full length to score with a flying header. Somebody wrote that I flew through the air like Superman. My most memorable game, of course, came in the same season when I scored all our nine goals in an FA Cup win at Margate. It was one of those crazy games when everything I touched turned to goals, and from that moment on my life was never quite the same again and people sat up and took notice of me.'

Ted MacDougall, his nine FA Cup goals in one match remain a record

Frank Swift, a huge man who seemed to fill the entire goal

THERE was a time when England was a treasure island of goalkeepers, and we were the envy of the world in the way we could produce a conveyor belt of top-flight goalies. Sad to say it is now all in the past tense, and too often our 'keepers are laughed at rather than lauded. I got to thinking which goalkeepers would be best equipped to stop the marksmen featured in my Top 50 from scoring. Here is a list of the Top 20 British goalkeepers of my lifetime, in date of birth order. I have slipped in just a couple of modern 'kepers to please and placate our younger readers.

Frank Swift

Born Blackpool, December 26 1913.

Died Munich, February 6 1958

Career span: 1932-49

League club: Manchester City (338 League appearances). England caps: 19

Jimmy Greaves assessment: He was the king of goalkeepers when I was a kid. The war robbed him of his peak years. Swiftie was a huge man who seemed to fill the entire goal. Ask any old pro and they will tell you he was one of the greatest 'keepers in history. Tragically, he was killed in the 1958 Manchester United air crash at Munich when travelling as a reporter for the *News of the World*.

Bert Williams

Born Bradley, Staffs, January 31 1920

Career span: 1937-1959

League clubs: Walsall (25 League games), Wolves (361). England caps: 24

Jimmy Greaves assessment: Nicknamed The Cat, Bert was the magnificent last line of defence for the Stan Cullis-managed Wolves team that dominated the 1950s. He was a perfectionist of a 'keeper without a weakness in his game, and he passed on many of his secrets when running a famous goalkeeping school. Bert was one of the first goalkeepers to perfect the art of distribution to launch counter-attacks.

Ted Ditchburn

Born Gillingham, October 24 1921

Died December 26 2005

Career span: 1946-58

League club: Tottenham (1946-58). England caps: 6

Jimmy Greaves assessment: I used to watch Ted play from the terraces, and was amazed at his agility and bravery. He would dive at the feet of forwards and gave as good as he got in barging battles when goalkeepers were not protected. Would have won many more caps but for the presence of the untouchable Swiftie.

Jack Kelsey

Born Llansamlet, Wales, November 19 1929

Died March 18 1992

Career span: 1949-63

League club: Arsenal (327). Wales caps: 41

Jimmy Greaves assessment: Stylish and a brilliant positional player, Jack was arguably the greatest goalkeeper to stand on the Arsenal goal-line. He was a master at knowing his angles, and was always commanding and in charge of his territory. Nobody knew the geometry and geography of the penalty area better than this proud Welshman.

Ronnie Simpson

Born Glasgow, October 11 1930

Died April 19 2004

Career span: 1946-70

League clubs: Queens Park (78), Third Lanark (21), Newcastle United (262), Hibernian (123), Celtic (118). Scotland caps: 5

Jimmy Greaves assessment: In an astonishing career that stretched nearly a quarter of a century, Ronnie was a hero on both sides of the border; He was twice an FA Cup winner with Newcastle United, and a decade later was the goalkeeper at the back of Jock Stein's history-making 1967 Euopean Cup-winning Celtic team. He had excellent positional sense and a safe pair of hands.

Bill Brown

Born Arbroath, October 8 1931

Career span: 1949-67

League clubs: Dundee (215), Tottenham (222), Northampton Town (17)

Scotland caps: 28

Jimmy Greaves assessment: I sometimes wondered if Bill was made of elastic as he stretched across goal to make saves in the days when I played with him at Tottenham. His positioning was often questionable, but he used to get himself out of trouble with instinctive saves. A quiet, unfussy goalkeeper who never seemed ruffled.

Ron Springett

Born Fulham, July 22 1935

Career span: 1953-68

League clubs: Queens Park Rangers (135), Sheffield Wednesday (345)

England caps: 33

Jimmy Greaves assessment: Ron was England's goalkeeper until the emergence of Gordon Banks. He was a reliable last line of defence who played in the 1962 World Cup and was in the 1966 squad. Ron was involved in a unique swap deal that took his younger goalkeeping brother Peter to Sheffield Wednesday when Ron returned to QPR. He was Mr. Reliable, with a commanding presence.

Eddie Hopkinson

Born Wheatley Hill, Co. Durham, October 29 1935

Died April 25 2004

Career span: 1952-70

League clubs: Oldham Athletic (3), Bolton Wanderers (519)

England caps: 14

Jimmy Greaves assessment: Hoppy was England goalie when I made my international debut in 1959, and I got a close-up view of his ability. He was a squat man, but was so agile and daring that he made up for lack of inches with excellent catching and positioning. The last line in a Bolton defence that was the toughest in the League. I have bruises on my memory to prove it.

Gordon Banks

Born Sheffield, December 30 1937

Career span: 1955-77

League clubs: Chesterfield (23), Leicester City (293), Stoke City (194)

England caps: 73

Jimmy Greaves assessment: Banskie was voted second greatest 'keeper of the 20th Century, with only the legendary Lev Yashin ahead of him. There was just a fingertip between them, and when I looked back and saw Banskie standing on the England goal-line I knew we were in safe hands. Even when he lost an eye in a car crash, he was better than most other goalies.

Peter Bonetti

Born Putney, September 27 1941

Career span: 1960-86

League clubs: Chelsea (495), Chelsea (105), Dundee United (5),

England caps: 7

Jimmy Greaves assessment: Catty is unfairly remembered for his cock-ups in the 1970 World Cup quarter-final, when he came in at the last minute for Gordon Banks after weeks without a match. He was one of the best catchers of a ball in the business and had lightning reflexes and great agility. Unlucky to live in Banksie's shadow.

Alex Stepney

Born Mitcham, Surrey, September 18 1942

Career span: 1961-79

League clubs: Millwall (137), Chelsea (1), Manchester United (433)

England caps: 1

Jimmy Greaves assessment: Alex would have got a cupboard-full of caps if Peter Shilton and Ray Clemence had not been around at the same time. He was safe and reliable at the back of the brilliant Manchester United defence when they won the European Cup at Wembley in 1968. His fantastic late save in ordinary time stopped Eusebio stealing the Cup for Benfica.

Gordon Banks, second only to Russian goalkeeping legend Lev Yashin

Pat Jennings, saving at the feet of his fellow Irishman George Best

Bob Wilson

Born Chesterfield, October 30 1941

Career span: 1962-74

League club: Arsenal (234)

Scotland caps: 2

Jimmy Greaves assessment: Willow was a key man in the Arsenal team that won the League title and FA Cup double in 1970-71, and became the first English-born player to be capped by Scotland. He had bravery to go with his ability, and often came to Arsenal's rescue with courageous dives at the feet of forwards. An intelligent man who used brain power to become a better player.

Pat Jennings

Born Newry, County Down, June 12 1945

Career span: 1963-86

League clubs: Watford (48), Tottenham (472) and Arsenal (237)

Northern Ireland caps: 119

Jimmy Greaves assessment: Pat, the man with the hands as big as shovels, was unquestionably the best goalkeeper I played with at club level. Cucumber cool and with the reflexes of a cobra, he covered his goal like a mountain from Mourne in his beloved County Down. It was a pleasure and a privilege to play with the big feller.

Ray Clemence

Born Skegness, August 5 1948

Career span: 1965-88

League clubs: Scunthorpe United (48), Liverpool (665), Tottenham (240)

England caps: 61

Jimmy Greaves assessment: Evidence of Ray's great talent, is that he managed to gather 61 England caps while of the same generation as the imperious Peter Shilton. He was a magnificent goalkeeper for the Liverpool team that threw a blanket over Europe in the 1980s and then brought his compusure to the Tottenham goal-line.

Peter Shilton

Born Leicester, September 18 1949

Career span: 1965-96

League clubs: Leicester City (266), Stoke (110), Nottingham Forest (202), Southampton (188), Derby (175), Plymouth (34), Bolton (1), Orient (9)

England caps: 125

Jimmy Greaves assessment: Physically imposing, Shilts was the king of consistency. You could count his bad games on the fingers of the Venus de Milo. He started as an understudy to Banksie and learned well from the master. His 125 England caps is a record that may never be beaten. Thank goodness, he moved more niftily on the goal-line than the dancefloor!

Phil Parkes

Born Sedgley, Staffs, August 8 1950

Career span: 1968-90

League clubs: Walsall (52), Queens Park Rangers (344), West Ham United (344), Ipswich Town (3). England caps: 1

Jimmy Greaves assessment: Big Phil looked as big on his goal-line as the wardrobes he now makes as a master carpenter. He is a legend in both West and East London, adored by fans at both clubs for whom he played exactly the same amount of League games. He was a superb shot-stopper and always had command of his box.

Neville Southall

Born Llandudno, Wales, September 16 1958

Career span: 1980-2002

League clubs: Bury (39), Everton (578), Port Vale (9), Southend United (3), Stoke City (12), Torquay United (53), Bradford City (1). Wales caps: 93

Jimmy Greaves assessment: Neville challenges Jack Kelsey as the greatest Welsh goalkeeper of all-time. He seemed as wide as he was tall, and bossed his penalty area with a mixture of skill and controlled physical power. Holds the appearances record for both Everton and Wales, which speaks volumes for his stability and safety.

Peter Shilton, the king of consistency with England

David Seaman, kept blank sheets galore for Arsenal

David Seaman

Born Rotherham, September 19 1963

Career span: 1982-2004

League clubs: Peterborough (91), Birmingham City (75), Queens Park Rangers (141), Arsenal (405), Manchester City (19). England caps: 75

Jimmy Greaves assessment: The anthem '1-0 to the Arsenal' sung throughout George Graham's managerial stay at Highbury owed much to the goalkeeping of David Seaman, who kept blank sheets galore. He was the second-most capped England goalkeeper after Peter Shilton, and had impressive physical presence as well as quick reflexes.

David James

Born Welwyn Garden City, August 1 1970

Career span: 1988 - present.

League clubs: Watford (89), Liverpool (214), Aston Villa (67), West Ham (91), Manchester City (93), Portsmouth (134), Bristol City (5 at time of publication)

England caps: 53

Jimmy Greaves assessment: Unfortunate to pick up the nickname 'Calamity James' because of some headline-hitting blunders, he is a class act when on top of his game. He makes difficult saves look easy, and commands his goal area with confidence and determination. The best of recent England goalkeepers.

Joe Hart

Born Shrewsbury, April 19 1987

Career span: 2003 - present.

League clubs: Shrewsbury Town (54), Manchester City 54 at time of publication), Tranmere Rovers (6), Blackpool (5), Birmingham City (36)

England caps: 7 (and counting)

Jimmy Greaves assessment: The most promising of the present squad of home-grown goalkeepers, who looks as if he can carry on the great tradition of his predecessors. I thought the same of Rob Green, until he made his confidence-wrecking blunder at the 2010 World Cup against the USA. Hart has kept the magnificent Shay Given on the City bench, which means he must be special.

JIMMY never bothered counting his goals. He left that to others. "I was too busy scoring them to count them," he says with that trademark cheeky smile of his. Sports statistician Michael Giller has been doing some adding up while playing the Greavsie numbers game. These were the goals that counted ...

357 goals in the First Division, an all-time record that will never be beaten because the division no longer exists (and don't forget he was being kicked and hacked by the likes of Chopper Harris, Norman 'Bites Yer Legs' Hunter, Nobby 'The Toothless Tiger' Stiles and Tommy 'The Anfield Iron' Smith, none of whom would last one minute in today's gentle, sanitized game).

44 goals in 57 England matches, just five behind the all-time record of Bobby Charlton in 106 appearances.

SIX TIMES First Division leading marksman, another record.

SEVEN First Division hat-tricks, **SIX** hat-tricks for England.

124 League goals for Chelsea (1957-61), then a club record.

220 League goals for Tottenham (1961-70), still a club record.

13 goals for West Ham (1970-71), **9** goals for AC Milan (1961)

Greavsie versus Lev Yashin in the 1963 England v the Rest of the World match at Wembley

35 goals in the FA Cup, and top scorer for his club in **12** of the 14 seasons in which he played in the First Division. **266 goals** in 379 Tottenham matches

491 goals in all matches at the time of his retirement from League football in 1971 at the all-too early age of 31, and not counting the dozens of goals he scored in non-League football.

Jimmy's most prolific goalscoring season was with Chelsea in 1956-57, while still an apprentice professional. He scored 114 goals and Chelsea presented him with an illuminated address to mark the feat. On the first day of the following season, he made his League debut and scored for Chelsea against Spurs at White Hart Lane. It was the start of the great goal rush.

JIMMY scored what was by any standards quite a goal for Tottenham against Manchester United at White Hart Lane on October 16 1965. It was voted 'Goal of the Decade' in a 1960s poll of players and public in the *Daily Express*. Among the top pros of the time who selected the goal as the greatest they had seen were George Best, Johnny Haynes, Geoff Hurst, Denis Law, Francis Lee, Martin Peters, Bruce Rioch, Terry Venables and Frank Worthington. Best and Law played in the game for United, and the rest saw the goal on television, and until the advent of colour television in 1970 it featured in the opening credits of the BBC's *Match of the Day* programme.

So what was so special about the goal that came during a stunning 5-1 dismantling of United, who were the reigning League champions? This is how a rather impressed Geoffrey Green, doyen of football writers, described it in *The Times*:

> Magic may be an overworked word. But what came next was just that. It was Greaves who set the high point to the banquet. Receiving from Mackay with his back to the United goal some 35 yards out, he sold two dummies, changed direction and in the bat of an eyelid had shimmied through and past the converging tackles of Foulkes, Stiles and Dunne. To get past one of these exceptional defenders is worthy of note. To go past all three in the space of a hall carpet is worth an illuminated address. There was still work to be done. Next, Greaves drew out the goalkeeper and bypassed him too, before stroking the ball into the gaping mouth of the net. The White Hart Lane ground erupted; the terraces waved like a forest in a gale, and Manchester United's players and supporters could only stand and wonder at it. This was the act of a Pele under the Brazilian skies, Monet making his best impression, Shostakovich composing a concerto. Greaves, the Fagin of the football field, the arch pickpocket of the penalty area, has stolen many spectacular goals but none quite so richly embroidered as this one.

The after-match comments from the United players who had been on the receiving end were a chrous of acclaim for the goal. 'No defence in the world could have stopped him,' said Nobby Stiles. 'We all knew we shouldn't have committed ourselves to tackles against him, but he draws you towards the ball like a bee to honey. You make your challenge and find yourself tackling thin air.'

Nobby Stiles, Manchester United's 'Toothless Tiger' who literally marked Greavsie

Sir Matt Busby, knighted after lifting the European Cup in 1968

'It was a goal of pure genius,' said Pat Crerand. 'We all just shrugged our shoulders and got on with the game. When that little so-and-so makes up his mind to score there's little you can do about it but just feel privileged to see a master at work.'

George Best said: 'Even though it was a goal against us it brought a smile to our faces. We almost enjoyed watching it! In my time in football, I've not seen a better executed goal. Jimmy was in total command of the situation from the moment the ball arrived at his feet. He knew exactly what he was doing, and left a queue of defenders chasing his shadow. Jimmy is a genius.'

Matt Busby – this was before he was knighted – was celebrating the twentieth anniversary of taking charge at United. 'It was nice of Jimmy to give me that goal as an anniversary present,' he joked. 'I don't think I've seen a better goal scored against us. Jimmy is a master of fashioning a goal out of nothing. Only Denis Law can match him for turning a half-chance into a goal. We are very lucky to have players of their calibre in our game.'

Denis Law watched the moment of Greaves genius from the touchline bench, in this first season when substitutes were allowed. 'I had gone off injured and John Fitzpatrick was substituting for me,' said the original King of Old Trafford. 'Watching from the sidelines was like seeing poetry in motion. I have always considered Jimmy the greatest goalscorer of all-time and this is the goal that surely proves it. It was just magnificent.'

When did Jimmy make up his mind that he was going to score? This was his analysis:

•It was not premeditated. I didn't plan goals. I just waited for any chance that presented itself. It was purely an instinctive thing with me. With this particular goal I remember receiving the ball from Dave Mackay. John Fitzpatrick was breathing down my neck and I turned him, pretending to go off right but then setting off in a straight line. From then on everything's a bit of a blur in my memory. But I've seen the goal enough times on television to know that I changed direction two or three times to throw Nobby, Foulksie and Tony Dunne off balance. If I had any skill, that was it – the ability to wrong-foot opponents.

A goalscorer is like a card sharp. While you've got the ball at your feet you're holding all the cards. You know where you're going, and the objective is to kid the man or men in front of you that you're going somewhere else. So you set out to deceive them with little feints, sudden changes of direction and acceleration.

If you look at pictures of any of the great ball-playing marksmen scoring their goals you will usually see one or two defenders on the ground behind them. That's because they had a gift for making defenders commit themselves to tackles. It's

Jimmy at 17 on his way to his first League goal ... for Chelsea at Tottenham

like a boxer counter-punching. You wait for them to make the lead then, whoosh, you're off and past them before they can get their balance back.

I remember my very first goal in League football was for Chelsea against Tottenham at White Hart Lane in 1957. The papers ran a series of pictures showing my route to goal and in each picture there were Tottenham defenders on their arses. Just a few years earlier I had been a fan asking the Spurs players for their autographs.

I was never a whacker of a ball. I couldn't burst the skin of a rice pudding from fifteen yards. Power shooting is a different game altogether. You have to distribute your bodyweight in a different way. I was usually on my toes for my goals and I used to pass rather than shoot the ball into the net.

For that goal against United, I drew goalkeeper Pat Dunne off his line and let him think he was dictating the angle to me while I knew that I was really in charge. He was inviting me to shoot into the left-hand side of the goal and I dropped my shoulder and cocked my right foot to pretend I had accepted his invitation. I waited until he had all his weight on his left-hand side and then moved wide of him and was left with the simple task of steering the ball into the net. By talking about the goal I have made it sound as if it were some carefully thought-out creation, while it was all over in a flash. I had played it completely off-the-cuff.

People are always reminding me of that goal, but I honestly think I scored a better one against Leicester a couple of years later at the Lane. It was similar to the United goal, but what made it even more satisfying was that I collected the ball from a clearance by Pat Jennings. So it was literally an end-to-end move, with only two of us touching the ball. It was not route one, because I had to outwit a line of Leicester defenders before I slipped the ball past the oncoming Peter Shilton, who was later kind enough to call it the best goal ever scored against him.'

There is one other goal that Jimmy puts above even his magical strikes against Manchester United and Leicester. 'The goal that gave me greatest satisfaction came after I had retired from playing League football,' he said, just a little tongue-in-cheek. 'It was a non-League match for Barnet at Underhill in the closing days of my career.

'I was playing as a Gunter Netzer-type midfield schemer and rarely got into the box. I volleyed a shot from 35 yards that flew into the top corner of the net. Nobody could believe it, including me. It was the hardest shot I ever hit in my life, and a collectors' item because I had rarely scored from outside the box.'

We had to bend Jimmy's arm to get him to talk in any depth about goalscoring. Throughout his career he would always say that the most important goal was his *next* one, and would insist that any ball that crossed the goal-line was good in his book. As the uncrowned king of goalscorers he deserves the last word on the subject of goals, and we know it will be echoed by all marksmen: 'A goal is a goal is a goal.'

EXTRA-TIME: Tribute to the King

WHILE it is never easy to get Jimmy talking about his own gathering of goals, he is always comfortable speaking in praise of other goalscorers, as he has proved with his expert assessments. We asked him to name his greatest non-British goalscorer and he had no hesitation in coming up with the legendary name Pelé. This is his tribute to The King:

```
FACTFILE: Born Tres Coracoes, Brazil, October 23 1940
Career span: 1955-77
Clubs: Santos 1955-74 (605 League games, 589 goals), New
York Cosmos 1975-77 (64 games, 37 goals). Club honours:
13 Brazilian league titles. Brazil: 92 caps (77 goals).
World Cup winners' medals 1958, 1962 (did not play in
the final), 1970. Voted Athlete of the 20th Century by
the Olympic Association in 1999. Named Footballer of the
Century by Fifa in 2000 (shared with Maradona). In all
competitions, Pelé scored a total of 1,281 goals.
```

Let me tell you about the twenty minutes I once spent in the company of one Edson Arantes do Nascimento, better known to you perhaps as Pelé. Well, I say 'spent in his company'. In truth, I spent the twenty minutes chasing his arse.

It was during a four-team tournament in Rio de Janeiro to celebrate the 50th anniversary of the Brazilian FA back in 1964. The other teams taking part were Argentina and Portugal. We, England that is, got the short straw and were drawn to play reigning world champions Brazil in the opening match in front of 150,000 screaming fans at the magnificent Maracana Stadium.

Our manager Alf Ramsey came up with this cunning plan designed to paralyse Pelé, in what was his peak period as the greatest player on the planet. 'We will stop the ball getting to him,' he said simply in the pre-match tactics talk.

Then – turning to his 'hard-tackling' inside-forwards – he added: 'Jim (little old me) and George ('Matchstick Man' Eastham), I want you to drop back whenever necessary, and help Gordon (Milne) and Bobby (Moore) to cut out the passes meant for him.'

'Anything you say, Alf,' I agreed. It seemed a good idea on paper, but would it work on the pitch? Stop the ball getting to Pelé. Even the Master couldn't play without the ball. Nice one, Alf.

The plan worked to perfection for the first 40 minutes, but then just before half-time a frustrated Pelé at last got possession and threaded the ball through to a young

The King celebrates in the arms of Jairzinho

Art Turner
2010

Sir Alf Ramsey, who had a plan to stop Pelé

newcomer called Rinaldo, who whipped the ball first time past our goalkeeper Tony Waiters. *Brazil 1, England 0.*

Despite this late set-back, we felt satisfied with our first-half performance and Alf demanded more of the same in the second-half. 'You're every bit as good as they are,' he said, with that steely eyed confidence we were to get to know so well on the way to the 1966 World Cup finals. 'Just keep working, and remember – don't let Pelé have the ball.'

This was the equivalent of saying 'don't let Louis Armstrong sing' ... 'don't let Neil Armstrong walk on the moon' ... 'don't let Lance Armstrong ride his bike.' But it was a good plan.

It got even better early in the second-half, when I pounced on a loose ball in the Brazilian penalty area and stuffed it into the back of their net. Suddenly in the Maracana you could have heard a pin or a pun drop, and it was England who were laughing.

Alf on the touchline bench grinned like the cat that had got the cream, and waved his fists to call for more of the same.

The game was now more than an hour old. *Brazil 1, England 1.* Budgie Byrne and I put shots inches wide, and goalkeeper Gilmar had to become an acrobat to tip a George Eastham shot on to the bar. Pelé was nowhere to be seen. Alf's cunning plan was working like a dream ... and it was England who were dreaming of a victory.

Then, like a black panther coming out of a sleep, Pelé roared into the game as if he had been deliberately sitting it out while he weighed up what we had in our locker.

First, with me chasing his arse and failing to stop the ball reaching him, he went this way, that way and then – after making a pretence at shooting – passed the ball again to Rinaldo, whose rising, whiplash left foot shot gave Tony Waiters no chance. *Brazil 2, England 1.*

'Who the f*** is this Rinaldo?' George Cohen gasped, doing his best to mark and contain a player none of us had ever heard of.

Moments later I had a shot scrambled off the Brazilian goal-line. The ball was cleared to Pelé, who set-off on a magical carpet ride through the England defence. He ran fully 40 yards with the ball at his feet, going past tackles as nonchalantly as if he was knocking aside daisies. He looked up and picked his spot before beating Tony Waiters all ends up with a fiercely hit right foot shot. Poor old Tony, a Blackpool beach lifeguard in his spare time, was in danger of drowning. *Brazil 3, England 1.*

We had forgotten Plan A. Don't let Pelé have the ball.

Now the Maracana was a madhouse. Ever heard 150,000 Brazilians screeching their heads off? It's like standing on the runway at Heathrow. Bobby Moore, who was in danger of getting a sunburned tongue from chasing Pelé, shouted something to me, but all I could see was his lips moving. He later revealed he was saying, 'Come back and help us mark f***** Pelé.'

Within two minutes of this third goal, Tony Waiters was picking the ball out of his net again. Pelé, of course, was the instigator. George Cohen was protesting to the referee about two Brazilian players being in offside positions when Pelé pushed a pass into the path of Julinho. The flag should have gone up as he slotted the ball wide of Waiters. But perhaps the linesman didn't fancy upsetting the frenzied fans baying behind him. In his shoes I wouldn't have been brave enough to raise the offside flag. *Brazil 4, England 1.*

In fifteen minutes of sheer brilliance, Pelé had turned the game on its head. And he still hadn't finished. I was again chasing that arse of his (what muscular buttocks, almost animal-like) when Bobby Moore ran across his path and conceded a free-kick a yard outside the box.

Pelé dummied as if to take the free-kick, and then Dias ran in alongside him and chipped the ball wide of a despairing dive by Waiters, who would have much preferred at that moment to be diving off Blackpool beach. *Brazil 5, England 1.*

We just could not believe what had happened to us as the referee blew the final whistle. No, that's silly. We did know what had happened to us. Pelé had happened to us. We had let him have the bloody ball.

I can honestly say that the football he produced in those final twenty minutes was the greatest I had ever witnessed in my life from an individual. I knew I had seen something special that, one day, I could tell my grandchildren about. That day is now, and the memory of it still sings in my head. While it hurt at the time, the pain has long gone and the beauty of it is what remains. I know that on that afternoon in the Maracana Stadium in Brazil I had been in the presence of sheer genius.

For that twenty minutes of magic alone I would have Pelé top of my all-time list of great footballers. But he did manage a thing or two besides, like scoring 1,218 goals in 1,363 matches from his debut at the age of fifteen until his first retirement on October 2 1974, 21 days short of his 34th birthday.

His peak year for goals was 1958 when he scored the little matter of 139 times, including two classic goals in the World Cup final when we first became aware of the developing legend that was Pelé. He went on to collect 12 goals in four World Cup final tournaments, and he remains the only player to have been a member of three World Cup winning teams (1958/62/70), although he missed the final stages of the 1962 tournament because of a pulled muscle. European clubs queued to try to buy him but the Brazilian government, fearing street riots, declared him a National Treasure so that he could not be taken abroad.

Born on the poverty line in Tres Coracoes in the same year as me, 1940, he came under the influence of former Brazilian World Cup player Waldemar de Brito while playing for his local team Noroeste. De Brito, realising he had unearthed a diamond, whisked him off to Santos in Sao Paulo, where he made a scoring first-team debut at the age of fifteen. A year later, at sixteeen, he was in the Brazilian international team, and the following year became at seventeen the then youngest ever World Cup debutant. The rest, as they say, is history.

Art Turner
2010

Pele, who provided the kiss of death for England in a 5-1 rout

Bobby Moore, who was prophetic about Argentina captain Antonio Rattin

Pelé was no angel, by the way, despite his carefully cultivated public personna. There was quite a bit of devil in him. Let me tell a story to illustrate just how competitive he could be:

After the match in which he took us apart in Rio, we flew up to Sao Paulo to watch the second match of the 'mini-World Cup' between Brazil and Argentina, and I can say hand-on-heart that I have never witnessed scenes like it. Because there were no seats left in the stand, the entire England party – including players, journalists and officials – were assigned to touchline benches that were just two yards from the pitch and eight or so yards from the fenced-in capacity crowd.

It was far too close for comfort.

As soon as we sat down the spectators spotted us and set up a deafening chant of 'Cinco-Uma!' – Portuguese for five-one – and a derisive reminder of our defeat in Rio (when we foolishly let Pelé have the ball). Born joker Budgie Byrne could not resist the bait and stood up on the bench and started conducting the fans like the man in the white suit before the old Wembley Cup finals. The Brazilians loved it and started chanting in time to Budgie's waving arms.

Budgie's choir switched their attention to cheering the Brazilian team when they came out on the pitch, and they lit up the night sky by firing three-stage firework rockets high above the stadium. Then we had fireworks of a different kind on the pitch.

Right from the first whistle Argentinian hatchet-man defender, Messiano, made it clear that his one intention was to stop Pelé from playing. He was not only going to stop him having the ball, but was also determined to give him a good kicking. It was a duel that underlined the naked hatred between Brazil and Argentina.

Messiano kicked Pelé at every opportunity, tripped him, spat at him, wrestled him to the floor and pulled his shirt anytime he seemed likely to get past him. Finally, after about thirty minutes of this almost criminal assault, the devil came out of Pelé as he completely lost his temper.

Right in front of us on the touchline bench, he took a running jump at Messiano and butted him full in the face. It made Zinedine Zidane's head-butt in the 2006 World Cup final seem like a harmless kiss.

The Argentinian was carried-off with his broken nose splattered across his face, and – incredibly – the Swiss referee allowed Pelé to play on. He knew that if he had ordered him off there would have been crowd riots. The giant Antonio Rattin then took over the marking job, and trod all over Pelé to the point where my best pal Bobby Moore said to me: 'Rattin is a genius of a player, but he thinks he can referee the match.' How prophetic those words were to prove.

The calculated, cynical fouling by the Argentinians had knocked all the rhythm and style out of the Brazilians, and the stadium became as quiet as a morgue when two minutes from the end, Telch, the player substituting for the flattened Messiano scored his second goal of the match to make it 3-0 to Argentina.

Budgie Byrne unwisely chose this moment to do an insane thing. He stood on the bench again to face the fans and, holding up three fingers, invited them to join in a chant of 'Three-Zero ...' It was the worst joke of Budgie's life. Suddenly bricks and fireworks rained down from the terraces as the fans turned their disappointment on us. They would have much preferred to reach the detested Argentinians but we were nearer targets.

The usually impassive Alf Ramsey took one wide-eyed look at the avalanche of rubble, rubbish and rockets coming our way and gave his shortest ever tactical talk. 'Run for it lads ...'

Luckily the final whistle had blown and we made a mad dash for the safety of the centre-circle. Villain Budgie Byrne then turned hero as his quick wits finally got us off the pitch in one piece. As the fans began to scream blue murder despite the intimidating presence of armed police, Budgie shouted the wise instruction: 'Grab yourself a Brazilian player.'

He then seized goalkeeper Gilmar lovingly by the arm and walked him off the pitch, knowing full well that no fans would try to harm one of their idols. We all followed Budgie's lead and went off arm-in-arm with bewildered Brazilian players.

You may think we were over-reacting, but uppermost in the minds of everybody in the stadium was the fact that just ten days earlier 301 people had been killed in a riot at the national stadium in Peru where Argentina had been the opponents.

I think the way Argentina had played against Brazil that night – brutally and with deliberate violence aforethought – stayed imprinted on Alf Ramsey's mind and was one of the reasons he made his infamous 'animals' outburst against them after the 1966 World Cup quarter-final in which Rattin got his marching orders for trying to referee the match. Mooro was on the ball as usual.

Pelé, of course, got mercilessly kicked out of the 1966 World Cup, but got his old appetite back in time to steer the greatest of all the Brazilian teams to the 1970 World Cup triumph. He played on for four more years before announcing that his fantastic career was over.

In 1975 former *Daily Express* football writer Clive Toye, then general manager of New York Cosmos, persuaded Pelé to make a comeback in the North American Soccer League. He made a final final farewell appearance against his old club Santos in New Jersey before a sell-out 60,000 crowd on October 1 1977.

It was Pelé's one thousand, three hundred and sixty-third match and he naturally marked it with a goal to bring his career total to 1,281.

Anybody who knows me will understand that these stats are coming from football historians Norman and Michael Giller, who could both bore for Britain. I prefer to think in terms of flesh and blood rather than facts and figures, and what I can say with complete authority is that Pelé was the greatest footballer ever to grace a football pitch.

I know, because I once chased his arse.

EXTRA-TIME: Goals! Goals! Goals!

W E pride ourselves at A1 Sporting Books on always including the most significant statistics, provided by father-and-son sports historians Norman and Michael Giller. The table below gives the top 20 scorers in the Premier League since it kicked off in 1992-93.

1	Alan Shearer	260
2	Andy Cole	187
3	Thierry Henry	174
4	Robbie Fowler	163
5	Les Ferdinand	149
6	Michael Owen	148
7	Teddy Sheringham	147
8	Frank Lampard	130
9	J. Floyd Hasselbaink	127
10	Dwight Yorke	123
11	Robbie Keane	121
12	Nicolas Anelka	118
13	Ian Wright	113
14	Dion Dublin	111
15	Emile Heskey	107
16	Wayne Rooney	107
17	Ryan Giggs	104
18	Paul Scholes	102
19	Matt Le Tissier	101
20	Jermain Defoe	97

● Alan Shearer's haul included 58 penalties

Alan Shearer, the premier goalscorer

THESE are the main Premier League goalscoring records since the first season in 1992-93, correct up to the time of publication in October 2010:

FIRST GOAL: Brian Deane scored the first ever Premier League goal for Sheffield United against Manchester United at Bramall Lane on the opening day of the 1992-93 season. Time on the clock: five minutes. He also scored the second goal for the Blades in a 2-1 victory.

TOP MAN: Alan Shearer (260) is the only player to score 200 Premier League goals. Andy Cole (187) is his closest rival.

Mr CONSISTENCY: Manchester United's Ryan Giggs is the only player to score in all 19 Premier League seasons.

THE FASTEST: Ledley King scored the fastest ever Premier League goal, timed at 10.2 seconds in Tottenham's 3-3 draw with Bradford in 2000-01.

FIRST HAT-TRICK: Eric Cantona, playing for Leeds United, was the first player to score a hat-trick in the Premier League in the 5-0 victory over Tottenham at Elland Road on August 15 1992.

QUICKEST HAT-TRICK: Robbie Fowler scored the fastest Premier League hat-trick in four minutes 33 seconds for Liverpool against Arsenal at Anfield on August 28 1994.

FIRST TO FOUR: Efan Ekoku was the first player to score four goals in one Premier League match in Norwich City's 5-1 victory over Everton at Goodison Park on September 25 1993.

FIRST TO FIVE: Andy Cole was the first player to score five goals in a Premier League match, for Manchester United against Ipswich in the 1994-95 season. The final score was 9-0, also a Premier League record for the biggest victory/defeat. Only two other players have gone nap – Alan Shearer (Newcastle v Sheffield Wednesday 1999-2000) and Jermain Defoe (Tottenham, in a 9-1 victory over Wigan in 2009-10, all scored in the second-half).

MILESTONE: Les Ferdinand scored the Premier League's 10,000th goal in Tottenham's 4-0 win over Fulham in December 2001.

EIGHT IN A ROW: Manchester United's Ruud Van Nistlerooy holds the record for scoring in the most consecutive games – eight in a row during the 2001-02 season, beating Mark Stein's record of seven set with Chelsea in the 1993-94 season. Counting the goals he scored in the first two matches of the following season, he stretched his scoring sequence to ten Premier League games.

YOUNGEST: James Vaughan (16 years, 271 days) became the youngest Premier League goalscorer when he netted for Everton against Crystal Palace on April 10 2005.

OLDEST: Teddy Sheringham (40 years, 268 days) became the oldest Premier League goalscorer when he found the net for West Ham against Portsmouth on December 26 2006.

SUPER SUB: Ole Gunnar Solskjaer came off the bench to score four goals in the last 17 minutes of Manchester United's 8-1 hammering of Nottingham Forest at the City Ground on February 6 1999.

David Beckham, who has a magic wand of a right foot

MOST IN A SEASON 1: 34 by Andy Cole (Newcastle, 1993-94) and Alan Shearer (Blackburn Rovers, 1994-95) when there were 42 games.

MOST IN A SEASON 2: 31 Alan Shearer (Blackburn Rovers, 1995-96) and Cristiano Ronaldo (Manchester United, 2007-08) when there were 38 games.

THREE IN DEFEAT: Matthew LeTissier scored a hat-trick on the opening day of the 1995-96 season, but he still ended up on the losing side when Southampton were beaten 4-3 by Nottingham Forest.

THE LONG SHOTS
(Distances measured by the *BBC Match of the Day* team)
Longest range goal: Goalkeeper Paul Robinson – 88 metres (96 yards) (direct free-kick), for Tottenham v Watford on March 7 2007.

Longest range volley: Matthew Taylor – 42 metres (46 yards), for Portsmouth v Everton on December 9 2006.

Longest range from open play: Xabi Alonso – 59 metres (65 yards), for Liverpool v Newcastle United on September 20 2006.

The Beckham lob: David Beckham made national headlines for the first time on August 17 1996 when he scored with a deliberate lob-shot from a yard inside his own half for Manchester United against Wimbledon at Selhurst Park. The distance carried was 61 yards. It was the opening day of the 1995-96 season, and Becks has hardly been out of the headlines since.

GOALS FOR ALL SEASONS
The Premier League team records:

Most goals scored: **103**, Chelsea (2009-10)

Fewest goals scored: **20**, Derby County (2007-08)

Most goals conceded (42 games): **100**, Swindon Town (1993-94)

Most goals conceded (38 games): **89**, Derby County (2007-08)

Fewest goals conceded: **15**, Chelsea (2004-05)

Best goal difference: **+71**, Chelsea (2009-10)

Worst goal difference: **-69**, Derby County (2007-08)

Most goals scored at home: **68**, Chelsea (2009-10)

Most goals scored away: **47**, Manchester United (2001-02)

Fewest goals scored at home: **10**, Manchester City (2006-07)

Biggest home win: **9-0**, Man United v Ipswich (March 4 1995)

Biggest away: **1-8**, Nottingham Forest v Man United (Feb 6 1999)

Highest scoring: **7-4** Portsmouth v Reading (September 29 2007)

FROM the Premier League we move to the all-time goalscoring records, with a particular nod in the direction of Jack Rollin, Albert Sewell and Barry J. Hugman, three omniscient statisticians whose facts and figures we have studied (and stolen!) for more than thirty years. Thank you, gentlemen. We present the records in the order they were set ...

INDIVIDUAL

- Hat-tricks in one season: **9, George Camsell** (Middlesbrough, 1926-27)

- Goals in a season: **60, Dixie Dean** (39 matches, for Everton 1927-28)

- Career hat-tricks: **37, Dixie Dean** (Tranmere Rovers, Everton, 1923-1937)

- Youngest scorer: **Ronnie Dix, 15y 180d** (Bristol Rovers v Norwich, Mar 3 1928)

- Own goals in one season: **5, Bobby Stuart** (Middlesbrough, 1934-35)

- 'Old' First Division: **7, Ted Drake** (for Arsenal at Aston Villa Dec 14 1935)

- Goals in a game: **10, Joe Payne** (for Luton v Bristol Rovers, April 13 1936)*

- League goals: **434, Arthur Rowley** (1946-65)

- 'Old' First Division goals: **357, Jimmy Greaves** (1957-71)

- Fastest goal: **4 secs, Jim Fryatt** (Bradford P.A. v Tranmere, April 25 1964)

- Hat-trick: **2m 20s, James Hayter** (Bournemouth v Wrexham, Feb 23 2004)

- Fastest on debut: **7 secs, Freddy Eastwood** (Southend v Swansea, Oct 16 2004)

- Fastest by a substitute: **1.8s, Nicklas Bendtner** (Arsenal v Spurs Dec 22 2007)

- Headed hat-trick **8m 23s, Jordan Rhodes** (Huddersfield v Exeter, Oct 10 2009)

*Scored in a Third Division South match and for ever after Joe was known as 'Ten-goal' Payne .

Len Shackleton, the Clown Prince who scored six goals in a 13-0 debut match

TEAM RECORDS

● Record away win: **Port Vale 0, Sheffield U. 10** (Second Div, Dec 10 1892)

● Most League goals conceded: **141, Darwen** (Second Division, 1898-99)

● Home League goals scored: **87, Millwall** (Third Division South, 1927-28)

● Highest scoring draw: **6–6**: (Leicester City v Arsenal 6 (April 21 1930); Charlton Athletic v Middlesbrough (October 22 1960)

● 'Old' First Division goals scored in a season: **128, Aston Villa** (1930-31)

● Away League goals scored in a season: **60, Arsenal** (First Division, 1930-31)

● Most top table goals conceded: **125, Blackpool** (1930-31)

● Home league goals conceded: **63, Rochdale** (Third Division North, 1931-32)

● Record win, **13-0**: Stockport v Halifax (Third Division North, Jan 6 1934); Newcastle United v Newport County (Second Division, October 5 1946)*

● Most in a game: **17, Tranmere 13 Oldham 4** (Third Div. N., Dec 26 1935)

● Most goals scored by a losing side: **6 by Huddersfield Town** – 7-6 to Charlton Athletic (December 21 1957). Johnny Summers scored six of Charlton's goals.

● League goals scored in a season: **134, Peterborough** (Fourth Division, 1960-61)

● Consecutive games scoring: **55, Arsenal** (May 19 2001-November 30 2002)

● Fewest home goals in a season: **10, Manchester City**, (Premier, 2006-07)

● Fewest top table goals: **20, Derby County** (Premier League, 2007-08)

* Len Shackleton was making his debut for Newcastle and scored six of the 13 goals

ENGLAND'S TOP MARKSMEN
The Top 20 Table of post-war scorers

1   Bobby Charlton (1958-70) 106 Caps 49 Goals

2   Gary Lineker (1985-92) 80 Caps 48 Goals

3   Jimmy Greaves (1959-67) 57 Caps 44 Goals

4   Michael Owen (1998-2007) 89 Caps 40 Goals

5=   Tom Finney (1946-58) 76 Caps 30 Goals

5=   Nat Lofthouse (1950-58) 33 Caps 30 Goals

5=   Alan Shearer (1992-2000) 63 Caps 30 Goals

8   David Platt (1990-96) 62 Caps 27 Goals

9=   Bryan Robson (1981-89) 90 caps 26 goals

9=   Wayne Rooney (2003-) 68 caps 26 goals

11   Geoff Hurst (1966-71) 49 caps 24 goals

12   Stan Mortensen (1947-53) 25 caps 23 goals

13   Tommy Lawton (1938-48) 23 caps 22 goals

14=   Mike Channon (1973-77) 46 caps 21 goals

14=   Kevin Keegan (1974-81) 63 caps 21 goals

14=   Peter Crouch (2006-) 41 caps 21 goals

17=   Martin Peters (1966-73) 67 caps 20 goals

17=   Frank Lampard (2003-) 83 caps 20 goals

19   Steven Gerrard (2001-10) 88 caps 19 goals

20=   Johnny Haynes (1954-61) 56 caps 18 goals

      Roger Hunt (1962-67) 34 caps 18 goals

Kerry Dixon, the top scorer with 24 goals for Chelsea in 1984-85

EXTRA-TIME: All-time scoring records

THE following table shows the top League goalscorers since the Second World War, from the 'old' First Division (1946-1992) and bringing us up to date with all the leading marksmen in the Premier League (1992-2010).

1946-47: **Dennis Westcott** (Wolverhampon Wanderers) **37**

1947-48: **Ronnie Rooke** (Arsenal) **33**

1948-49: **Willie Moir** (Bolton Wanderers) **25**

1949-50: **Dickie Davis** (Sunderland) **25**

1950-51: **Stan Mortensen** (Blackpool) **30**

1951-52: **George Robledo** (Newcastle United) **33**

1952-53: **Charlie Wayman** (Preston North End) **24**

1953-54: **Jimmy Glazzard** (Huddersfield Town) **29**

1954-55 **Ronnie Allen** (West Bromwich Albion) **27**

1955-56: **Nat Lofthouse** (Bolton Wanderers) **33**

1956-57: **John Charles** (Leeds United) **38**

1957-58: **Bobby Smith** (Tottenham Hotspur) **36**

1958-59: **Jimmy Greaves** (Chelsea) **33**

1959-60: **Dennis Viollet** (Manchester United) **32**

1960-61: **Jimmy Greaves** (Chelsea) **41**

1961-62: **Ray Crawford** (Ipswich Town), **Derek Kevan** (WBA) **33**

1962-63: **Jimmy Greaves** (Tottenham Hotspur) **37**

1963-64: **Jimmy Greaves** (Tottenham Hotspur) **35**

1964-65: **Andy McEvoy** (Blackburn Rovers), **Jimmy Greaves** (Spurs) **29**

1965-66: **Willie Irvine** (Burnley) **29**

1966-67: **Ron Davies** (Southampton) **37**

1967-68: **George Best** (Man United), **Ron Davies** (Southampton) **28**

1968-69: **Jimmy Greaves** (Tottenham Hotspur) **27**

1969-70: **Jeff Astle** (West Bromwich Albion) **25**

1970-71: **Tony Brown** (West Bromwich Albion) **28**

1971-72: **Francis Lee** (Manchester City) **33**

1972-73 **Bryan (Pop) Robson** (West Ham United) **28**

1973-74: **Mike Channon** (Southampton) **21**

1974-75: **Malcolm Macdonald** (Newcastle United) **21**

1975-76: **Ted MacDougall** (Norwich City) **23**

1976-77: **Andy Gray** (Aston Villa), **Malcolm Macdonald** (Newcastle) **25**

1977-78: **Bob Latchford** (Everton) **30**

1978-79: **Frank Worthington** (Bolton Wanderers) **24**

1979-80: **Phil Boyer** (Southampton) **23**

1980-81: **Steve Archibald** (Tottenham), **Peter Withe** (Aston Villa) **20**

1981-82: **Kevin Keegan** (Southampton) **26**

1982-83: **Luther Blisset**t (Watford) **27**

1983-84: **Ian Rush** (Liverpool) **32**

1984-85: **Kerry Dixon** (Chelsea), **Gary Lineker** (Leicester City) **24**

1985-86: **Gary Lineker** (Everton) **30**

1986-87: **Clive Allen** (Tottenham Hotspur) **33**

1987-88: **John Aldridge** (Liverpool) **26**

1988-89: **Alan Smith** (Arsenal) **23**

1989-90: **Gary Lineker** (Tottenham Hotspur) **24**

1990-91: **Alan Smith** (Arsenal) **22**

1991-92: **Ian Wright** (Crystal Palace/Arsenal) **29**

Didier Drogba, twice a top Premier League marksman with Chelsea

PREMIER LEAGUE

42 games (1992-94); 38 games (1994-)

1992-93: **Teddy Sheringham** (Nottingham Forest/Tottenham) **22**

1993-94: **Andy Cole** (Newcastle United) **34**

1994-95: **Alan Shearer** (Blackburn Rovers) **34**

1995-96: **Alan Shearer** (Blackburn Rovers) **31**

1996-97: **Alan Shearer** (Newcastle United) **25**

1997-98: **Chris Sutton** (Blackburn Rovers), **Dion Dublin** (Coventry City),

Michael Owen (Liverpool) **18**

1998-99: **Michael Owen** (Liverpool), **Dwight Yorke** (Manchester United),

Jimmy Floyd Hasselbaink (Leeds United) **18**

1999-2000: **Kevin Phillips** (Sunderland) **30**

2000-01: **Jimmy Floyd Hasselbaink** (Chelsea) **23**

2001-02: **Thierry Henry** (Arsenal) **24**

2002-03: **Ruud Van Nistelrooy** (Manchester United) **25**

2003-04: **Thierry Henry** (Arsenal) **30**

2004-05: **Thierry Henry** (Arsenal) **25**

2005-06: **Thierry Henry** (Arsenal) **27**

2006-07: **Didier Drogba** (Chelsea) **20**

2007-08: **Cristiano Ronaldo** (Manchester United) **31**

2008-09: **Nicolas Anelka** (Chelsea) **19**

2009-10: **Didier Drogb**a (Chelsea) **29**